AF447417

THE INSANELY EASY GUIDE TO THE PIXEL TABLET

UNDERSTANDING HOW TO USE THE PIXEL TABLET

SCOTT LA COUNTE

RIDICULOUSLY

ANAHEIM, CALIFORNIA

www.RidiculouslySimpleBooks.com

Copyright © 2023 by Scott La Counte.

All rights reserved. No part of this publication may be reproduced, distributed or transmitted in any form or by any means, including photocopying, recording, or other electronic or mechanical methods, without the prior written permission of the publisher, except in the case of brief quotations embodied in critical reviews and certain other noncommercial uses permitted by copyright law.

Limited Liability / Disclaimer of Warranty. While best efforts have been used in preparing this book, the author and publishers make no representations or warranties of any kind and assume no liabilities of any kind with respect to accuracy or completeness of the content and specifically the author nor publisher shall be held liable or responsible to any person or entity with respect to any loss or incidental r consequential damages caused or alleged to have been caused, directly, or indirectly without limitations, by the information or programs contained herein. Furthermore, readers should be aware that the Internet sites listed in this work may have changed or disappeared. This work is sold with the understanding that the advice inside may not be suitable in every situation.

Trademarks. Where trademarks are used in this book this infers no endorsement or any affiliation with this book. Any trademarks (including, but not limiting to, screenshots) used in this book are solely used for editorial and educational purposes.

Disclaimer: *Please note, while every effort has been made to ensure accuracy, this book is not endorsed by Alphabet, Inc. and should be considered unofficial.*

Table of Contents

INTRODUCTION

As the digital landscape continues to evolve, the demand for powerful and versatile devices becomes even more prominent. When we think of a tablet, our minds may quickly drift to the popular iPad, yet there are alternatives that have proven to be robust contenders. This is where Google's Pixel Tablet enters the picture, rivaling the best of them with its potent combination of state-of-the-art design and superior performance.

The Pixel Tablet serves as a high-performing device that can compete with a range of portable computers, delivering a blend of mobile and desktop-like experiences. If you're new to the Pixel Tablet, you'll find this guide a valuable asset. We aim to uncover the layers of this sophisticated device, offering insights about its user interface, capabilities, and features.

The book is intended to cater to the needs of the everyday user, focusing on practical knowledge rather than complex technical information. If you're seeking to establish a firm understanding of your Pixel Tablet and explore its many functions, this is the guide for you.

In this book, we'll cover the following aspects of using your Pixel Tablet:

- Initial setup and personalization of your device
- Downloading and managing applications and widgets
- Connecting to Wi-Fi and managing network settings
- Customizing themes and wallpaper for a personalized look
- Navigating with Gestures for an intuitive user experience
- Taking advantage of the camera's features
- Browsing the Internet effectively and safely
- Adjusting system settings for optimal performance
- Exploring and understanding additional features like the Kids Mode
- And much more!

Ready to kickstart your Pixel Tablet journey? Let's dive right in! Note: This book is an independent publication and has not been authorized, sponsored, or otherwise approved by Alphabet, Inc.

[1]

START HERE

PIXEL TABLET VS. IPAD AIR (2022)

When it comes to comparing the Pixel against the iPad, there's a lot of comparison to make—Apple, afterall, has several iPad's to pick from. For the sake of this book, I will stack it up against the iPad Air from 2022, as it most closely aligns with the Pixels spec. Let's take a look.

DESIGN AND BUILD

The Pixel Tablet, sporting dimensions of 258 x 169 x 8.1mm, is slightly bulkier than the sleek iPad Air, which measures 247.6 x 178.5 x 6.1mm. The

Pixel is also heavier, weighing in at 493g compared to the Air's 461g. Both tablets feature a glass front, an aluminum frame, and aluminum back, meaning they both feel premium and durable.

If color variety tickles your fancy, the Pixel Tablet comes in Porcelain, Hazel, and Rose, while the iPad Air offers Space Gray, Starlight, Pink, Purple, and Blue.

DISPLAY

The Pixel Tablet features a larger 10.95-inch IPS LCD display compared to the iPad Air's 10.9-inch Liquid Retina IPS LCD. However, the iPad Air offers slightly better resolution, clocking in at 1640 x 2360 pixels (~264ppi), compared to the Pixel's 1600 x 2560 pixels (~276ppi). Either way, you're getting a crystal clear, vibrant display perfect for everything from work to Netflix binges on both tablets.

PERFORMANCE

Under the hood, the Pixel Tablet is powered by Google's own Tensor G2 chipset, while the iPad Air boasts Apple's powerful M1 chip. Both are blazingly fast, so performance shouldn't be an issue regardless of your choice. Also, both tablets offer 8GB of RAM, ensuring smooth multitasking. But if you're after more internal storage, the Pixel Tablet might just edge out the iPad Air, with options for 128GB and

256GB, compared to the Air's 64GB and 256GB offerings.

CAMERA AND SOUND

Both tablets come equipped with solid cameras. However, the iPad Air (2022) offers superior specs with a 12 MP main camera that can shoot video at 4K and a 12 MP ultra-wide selfie camera. The Pixel Tablet's camera, at 8 MP for both the main and selfie cameras, is less impressive on paper, though it should still suffice for casual photos and video calls.

When it comes to sound, both tablets boast stereo speakers for a premium audio experience. Unfortunately, neither offers a 3.5mm jack, so you'll have to rely on Bluetooth or a USB-C adapter for your headphones.

OPERATING SYSTEM

As expected, the Pixel Tablet runs on the latest Android 13, while the iPad Air operates on iPadOS 15.4, which is upgradable to iPadOS 16.5. Your preference here will likely come down to whether you're more comfortable in the Google or Apple ecosystem.

CONNECTIVITY AND BATTERY LIFE

In terms of connectivity, the Pixel Tablet only supports Wi-Fi while the iPad Air provides cellular connectivity options including GSM, HSPA, LTE, and even 5G. Both offer Wi-Fi 6 and Bluetooth, but only the iPad Air has GPS.

The battery situation is fairly comparable, with the Pixel packing a 27Wh battery and the iPad Air housing a slightly larger 28.6Wh unit. Exact life will vary depending on your usage, but both should get you through a typical day of use.

PRICE

When it comes to price, the Pixel Tablet comes in at around $499; the iPad Air is $599; expect occasional sales and discounts on each. The Pixel Tablet obviously also comes with a doc.

PIXEL TABLET VS. GOOGLE'S GALAXY TAB 8

Now let's look at Google's latest tablet. Since they both run Android, this will give you a better look at a tablet that has a similar ecosystem.

DESIGN AND BUILD

Starting with physical design, both the Pixel Tablet and Galaxy Tab 8 showcase the premium build quality we've come to expect from Google and Google. The Pixel Tablet measures 258 x 169 x 8.1mm and weighs in at 493g, while the Galaxy Tab

8 is slightly lighter and more compact, at 246.8 x 161.9 x 6.9mm and 508g.

When it comes to build materials, both tablets sport a glass front with an aluminum frame and back. The color options also differ, with the Pixel Tablet offering Porcelain, Hazel, and Rose, while the Galaxy Tab 8 comes in Gray, Silver, and Pink Gold.

DISPLAY

The Pixel Tablet boasts a larger 10.95-inch IPS LCD display with a resolution of 1600 x 2560 pixels. The Galaxy Tab 8, on the other hand, features a 10.5-inch TFT LCD display with a lower resolution of 1200 x 1920 pixels. The Pixel's higher resolution might make it a better choice for those who prioritize sharp, detailed visuals.

PERFORMANCE

The Pixel Tablet, running on Android 13 and powered by Google's own Tensor G2 chipset, is designed to provide top-tier performance. Its 8GB RAM should ensure smooth multitasking, and it comes with either 128GB or 256GB of internal storage.

The Galaxy S8 also comes with Android 13 and starts at 128GB of storage.

CAMERA AND SOUND

Both tablets offer good options for casual photography and video calls, though neither is aiming to replace your smartphone camera. The Pixel Tablet comes with 8 MP cameras on both the front and back, while the Galaxy Tab 8 offers an 12 MP rear camera and 4k video recording.

When it comes to audio, both tablets feature quad-speaker setups for a full, immersive sound. However, the Galaxy Tab 8 scores a point here with its 3.5mm jack, a feature absent from the Pixel Tablet.

CONNECTIVITY AND BATTERY LIFE

The Pixel Tablet supports dual-band Wi-Fi and Bluetooth 5.2 but lacks cellular connectivity. On the other hand, the Galaxy Tab 8 supports GSM, HSPA, and LTE cellular networks, as well as dual-band Wi-Fi and Bluetooth 5.0. It also has comprehensive positioning options including GPS, GLONASS, BDS, GALILEO, and QZSS.

In the battery department, the Galaxy Tab 8 is the clear leader, boasting a hefty 7040 mAh battery compared to the Pixel Tablet's 27 Wh unit.

PRICE

When it comes to pricing, the Pixel Tablet retails for about $499, a premium over the significantly cheaper Galaxy Tab 8, which costs around $699.

DELVING INTO THE WORLD OF ANDROID 13

In the ever-evolving world of operating systems, Android has proven time and time again to be a top contender. Never one to rest on its laurels, Google has once again upped the ante with its latest OS, Android 13. Let's dive into what makes this iteration unique, powerful, and more user-friendly than ever before.

UNDERSTANDING ANDROID 13

Hailed as one of the most significant overhauls in recent times, Android 13 is packed full of features and refinements that bring a whole new level of functionality and performance to compatible devices. With an emphasis on enhancing user experience, improving device management, and incorporating innovative AI technologies, Android 13 truly embodies Google's mission to make technology helpful for everyone.

ENHANCED USER EXPERIENCE

With Android 13, Google has taken strides to make your device more intuitive, personal, and responsive. Building upon Material You, Google's adaptable design language, Android 13 offers a customizable and interactive interface. Features like dynamic color picking from your wallpaper and widgets that better respond to your touch have taken center stage, adding a level of personalization that wasn't as prominent in previous iterations.

Furthermore, an improved notification management system helps users stay organized without feeling overwhelmed. Notifications are now grouped in a more logical manner, offering a streamlined, clutter-free experience.

ROBUST DEVICE MANAGEMENT

As our reliance on smart devices grows, so does the need for comprehensive and efficient device management. Recognizing this, Android 13 comes equipped with features like more efficient power usage, better app hibernation, and automatic resetting of app permissions for unused apps, ensuring your device stays secure and performs optimally.

ARTIFICIAL INTELLIGENCE (AI) AT ITS CORE

Google has long been a leader in AI technology, and Android 13 takes this commitment a step further. The latest AI features in Android 13 include more proactive suggestions and predictive actions, like faster auto-rotate screen orientations based on your face's position and smarter text selection. These improvements not only enhance the user experience but also demonstrate how Google is leveraging AI technology to make our devices smarter and more responsive.

INNOVATIVE ADDITIONS

Finally, Android 13 introduces some innovative additions like Ultra-Wideband (UWB) support. UWB is a short-range wireless communication protocol, like Bluetooth and Wi-Fi, that operates through radio waves. It offers spatial awareness capabilities – your device can understand its location in relation to other devices in real-time. This opens up a world of possibilities, such as more accurate direction sharing in Google Maps or finding your lost keys using a UWB-equipped tracker.

Android 13 is a leap forward in Google's quest to make technology more accessible, intuitive, and intelligent. As we delve deeper into this operating system in the coming months, we're sure to uncover even more ways that it's pushing the boundaries of what's possible in mobile technology. From smarter AI to more personalized experiences, Android 13 is indeed a game-changer. Stay tuned for more updates as we continue exploring this exciting frontier.

SETUP

The setup is pretty intuitive, but there are still screens that might confuse you a little. If you are a self-starter and like to just try things, then skip to the next section (Finding Your Way Around) on the main UI elements of Google. If you want a more thorough walk-through, then read away!

Google knows you want to get started using your tablet, so they've made the process pretty quick; most people will spend about 10 or 15 minutes.

The first thing you'll see is the "Welcome to your Pixel Tablet" screen. There's also an accessibly option, which will let you turn on adaptive controls if you are visually or hearing impaired. When you are ready to get started, tap the Get Started button

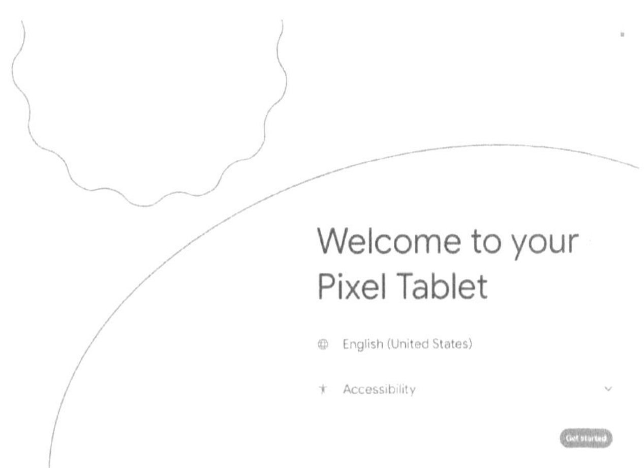

The firs thing you'll be ask to do is connect to wi-fi.

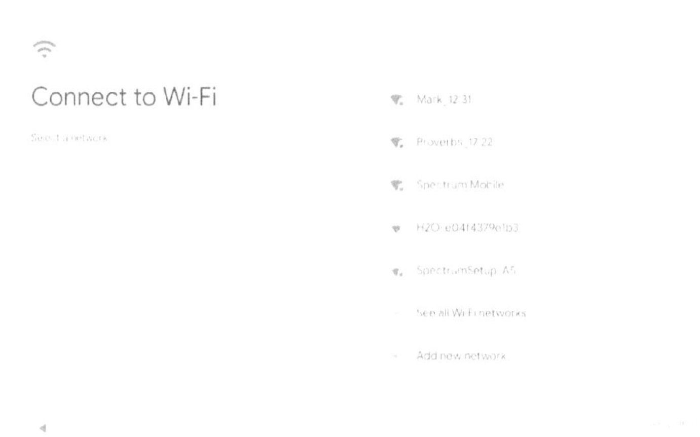

You'll notice there's a "Set up offline" option on the bottom. You don't technically need wi-fi to use your tablet or get it setup, but I highly recommend it because it will let the tablet check for updates—even if you get the tablet the first day it's released, there's usually updates you need to install.

The next screen is to copy apps and data; if you have an Android device (like a phone), then you might want to do this to help them sync up better and have similar apps. If you don't want to—or you don't have anything to copy from—then just click the Don't Copy button.

Remember that update I was talking about? That's the next thing that happens. You don't have to do anything…except wait. It typically will take one or two minutes, but could be a little longer.

Once your device is update, you'll have a chance to add in your Google account information. You don't have to (just tap Skip), but, again, I recommend it. This let's you check email on your tablet, as well as buy apps.

Once you get past the login screen, you reach the moment you've been waiting for: the terms and conditions. I'll spare you the details of what it says, and let you read through it yourself—with your lawyer, of course! Or you can do what 99.9999% of us do and agree to it blindly and hope for the best.

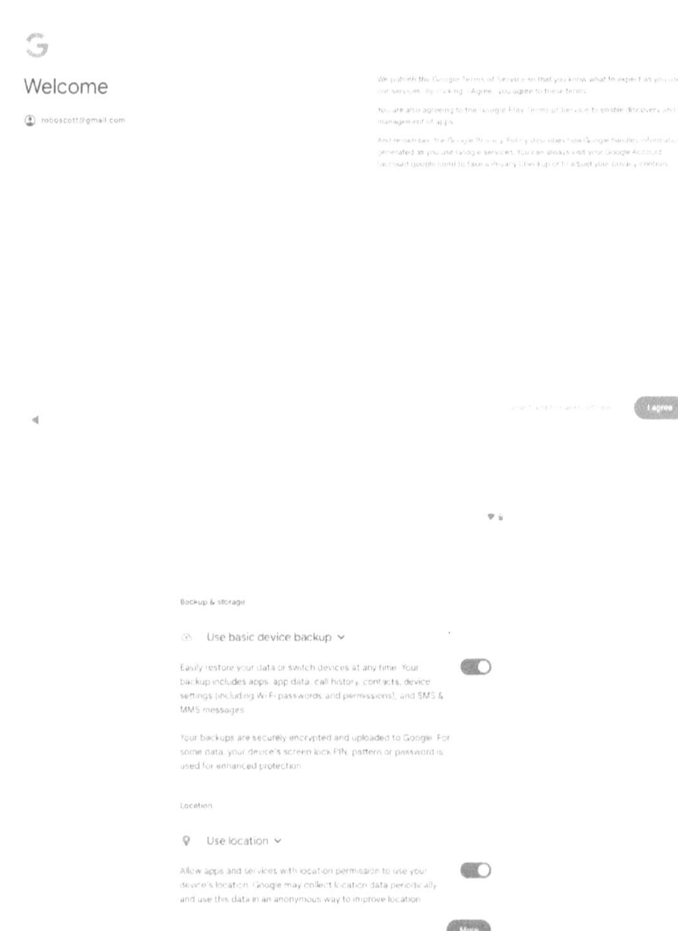
Welcome
roboscott@gmail.com
Backup & storage
Use basic device backup
Easily restore your data or switch devices at any time. Your backup includes apps, app data, call history, contacts, device settings (including Wi-Fi passwords and permissions), and SMS & MMS messages.
Your backups are securely encrypted and uploaded to Google. For some data, your device's screen lock PIN, pattern or password is used for enhanced protection.
Location
Use location
Allow apps and services with location permission to use your device's location. Google may collect location data periodically and use this data in an anonymous way to improve location
More

Once you get through those terms, go ahead and go to the next screen to see more of them!

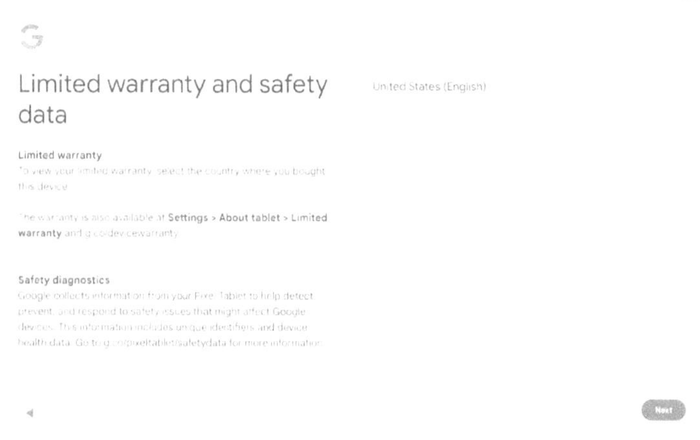

Finish reading all of them yet? Great! Because there's more!

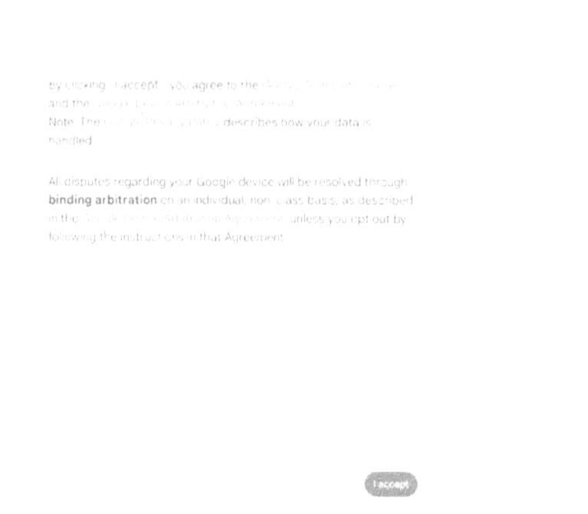

Did you enjoy all the legalize? We aren't done yet! Next is a screen about Google Assistant...along with the terms for it. Google Assistant is basically your personal AI robot who can help do things.

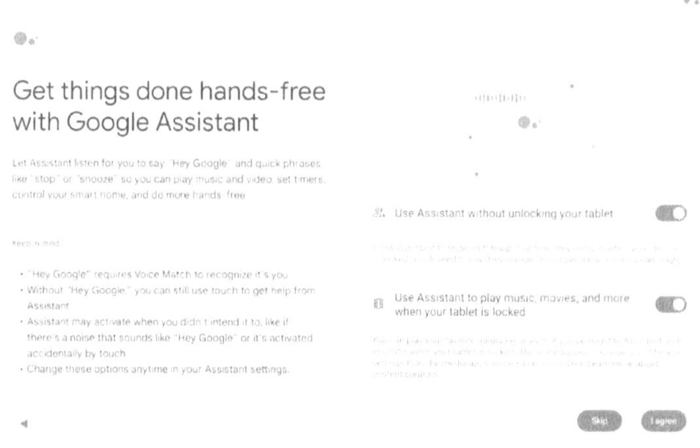

Once you agree or skip, there's more terms for you. This one is for "Hey Google"—this is Google's version of Siri on the iPhone—basically when you have questions you need to ask.

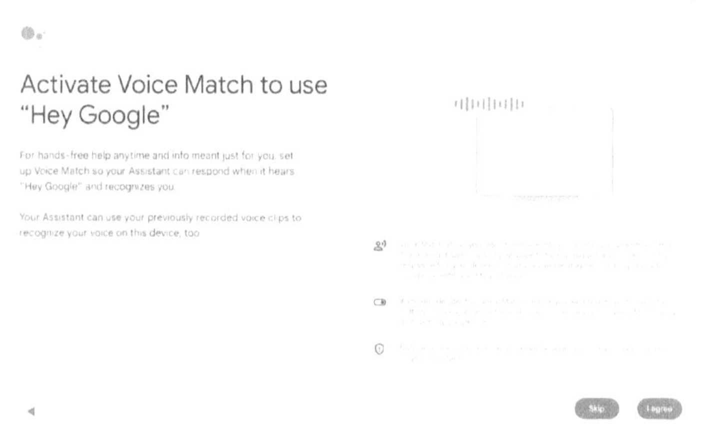

We are getting close to finishng! I'm sure your eager to use the tablet. The next screen let's you add extra customizations to your tablet. "No Thanks" let's you skip it.

Want to be on Pixel's marketing list and gets tips and tricks? Hit "Yes I'm in"…otherwise select, "No thanks."

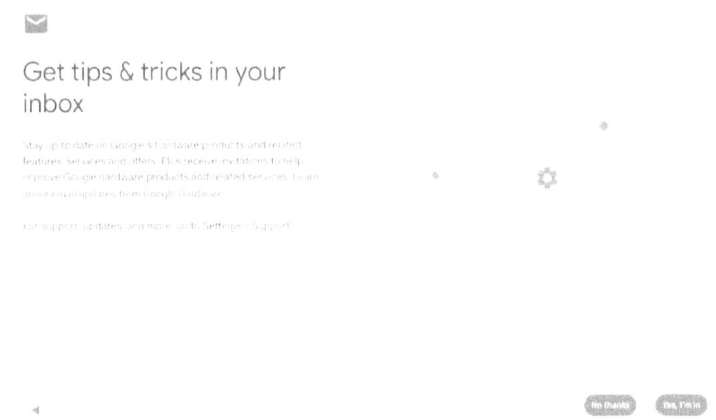

There's another loading screen next. You'll probably be here for a few seconds. It's just adding final tweaks to your tablet.

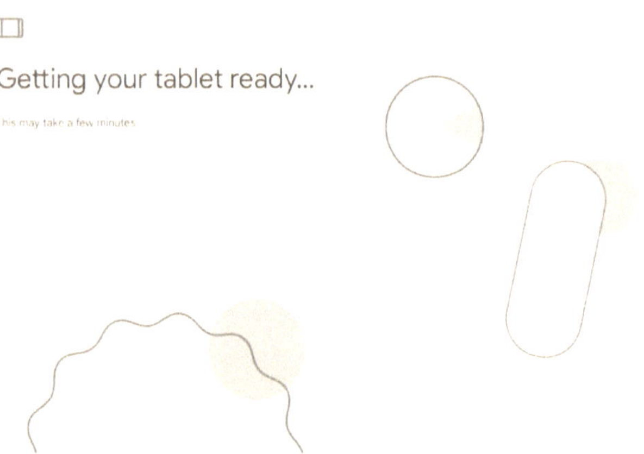

Once it's done, there's a quick tutorial on how to use the tablet. It takes about a minute and if you have never used a Google tablet, I recommend it, but you can also tap the Skip.

Finally, you reach the All Set screen! Your done! Just swipe up on the bottom of the screen, and you can now enjoy your tablet!

[2]
THE RIDICULOUSLY SIMPLE OVERVIEW

FINDING YOUR WAY AROUND

People come to the Pixel Tablet from all sorts of different places: iPad, other Android tablets, flip phone, two Styrofoam cups tied together with string. This next section is a crash course in the interface. If you've used Android before, then it might seem a little simple, so skip ahead if you already know all of this.

If any of this seems a little rushed, there's good reason: it is! We'll cover these points in more detail later. This is just a quick starter / reference.

When you see your main screen for the first time, you will see six components. They are: status icons, notifications, users, canvas, Google Search, and recent apps.

- **Notifications Bar** - This is a pull-down menu (slide down to expand it) and it's where you'll see all your alerts (new email or text, for example) and where you can go to change settings quickly.
- **Canvas** – on a desktop computer, this would be your desktop space; it's where you put all your app shortcuts and widgets (don't worry: we'll cover how to add things there later.

- **Google Search App** – The Google Search app is another example of a widget. As the name implies, it can search Google for information; but it also searches apps on your tablet.
- **Recent apps** – This row serves a dual purpose: it shows your recently used apps and it also lets you drag your favorite apps into the row, so they always appear.
- **Status icons –** this indicates if you have new email or notifications.
- **Users –** You can have multiple users on your Pixel Tablet; if you tap this button, it lets you quickly switch to the user using the tablet; everything will be there customized for them.

NOTIFICATIONS BAR

Next to the recent app bar, the area you'll use the most is the notification bar. This is where you'll get, you guessed it, notifications! What's a notification? That's any kind of notice you have elected to receive. A few examples: text message alerts, email alerts, amber alerts, and apps that have updates.

When you drag your finger down from the notification bar, you'll get a list of several settings that you can adjust. Press and hold any of these options and you'll open an app with even more options.

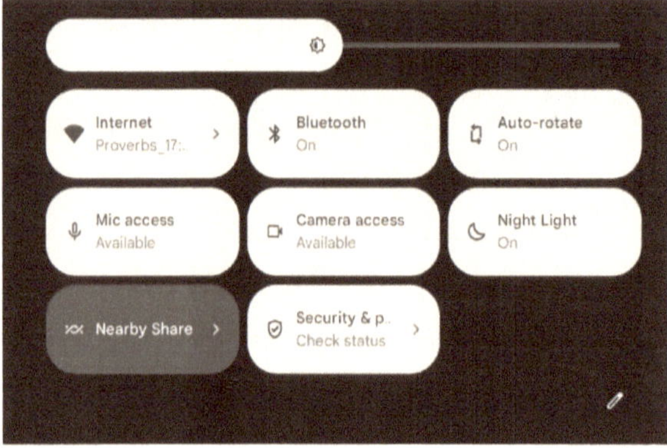

From right to left these are the options you can change or use:

- Internet
- Sound (tap to mute sounds)
- Bluetooth
- Lock the device from auto-rotating
- Airplane mode (which turns off wi-fi and Bluetooth)
- Power saving mode (which limits the speed of the tablets CPU and decreases the screen brightness to increase the battery life.
- Night mode to reduce the blue life.
- Nearby share
- Security

If you continue dragging down, this thin menu expands and there are a few more options.

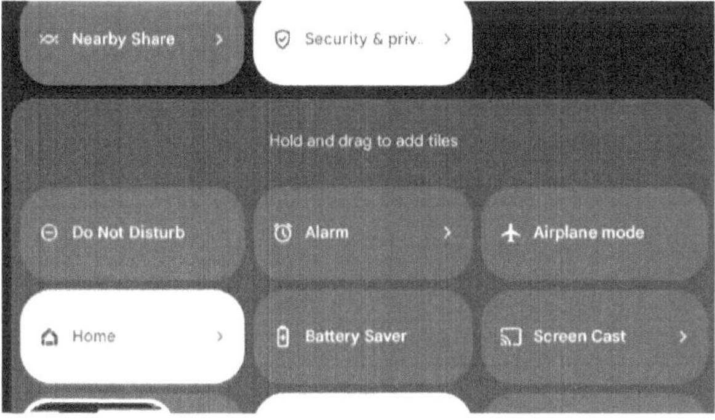

The first is at the bottom of the screen—it's the slider, and it makes your device brighter or dimmer depending on which way you drag it.

Above that, there are several controls. Many of these controls are just an on / off toggle, but some let you long press to see expanded options.

You can customize your notification area by long-pressing and dragging icons to move them around.

GETTING AROUND QUICKLY

Getting around your tablet is very much gesture based. What are those gestures?! Here's the big ones:

- Swipe up and release to get to your Home screen from any app.
- Swipe up and hold to bring up multitasking.

- Swipe right or left from the bottom edge of your screen to go backwards and forward.

You can change the gestures on your tablet by going into the settings app, then tapping on System > Gestures > System navigation.

You might recall that swiping up from the bottom showed you all your apps. That gesture now returns to the Home screen, so how do you see all your apps? From your Home screen, swipe up in the middle of the screen to see them.

Swiping up from the bottom will also bring up a launcher dock with your commonly used apps.

When it comes to getting around your Google, learning how to use gestures will be the quickest, most effective method. You can change some of the gesture options by going to System > Advanced features > Motion and gestures.

The most important gesture is how to get back to the Home screen—there are no buttons after all. That's the easiest one to remember: swipe up from the bottom of the screen.

MULTITASKING

Those are the easy gestures to remember; if you want to move around quickly, however, you need to know the two big multitask gestures, which help you switch between apps.

The first is to see your open apps. To do this, swipe up like you're going to the Home screen, but keep going until about the middle of the screen and then stop and lift your finger—don't make a quick swipe-up gesture like you would when going Home. This will show you previews of all of your open apps, and you can swipe between them. Tap the one you want to open.

The quickest way to switch back and forth between two or three apps, however, is to swipe from left to right along the bottom edge of the screen. This swipes between apps in the order that you have used them.

ZOOM

Need to see text bigger? There are two ways to do that. Note: this works on many, but not all apps.

The first way is to pinch to zoom.

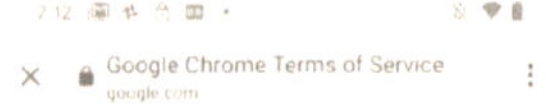

r with the Additic
between you an
es. It is importan
Collectively, this l
s".

etween what the
al Terms say, ther
elation to that Se

The second way is to double tap on the text.

ROTATE

You probably have noticed if you rotate your tablet, it rotates the screen. What if you don't want to rotate the entire screen? You can turn that off very easily. Swipe down and then tap the "arrows" button to enable or disable it.

HUB MODE

The Pixel Tablet is a pretty snazzy little device—but you probably didn't buy it because it was snazzy. You bought it because you saw it snap magically to the that speaker dock and essentially become a Google Home.

It's a simple feature—one that makes you say, "Why hadn't someone else thought of that?" But for as simple as it is, there's a lot you can customize.

To get started, open up the Settings app, then tap on Hub Mode on the left panel.

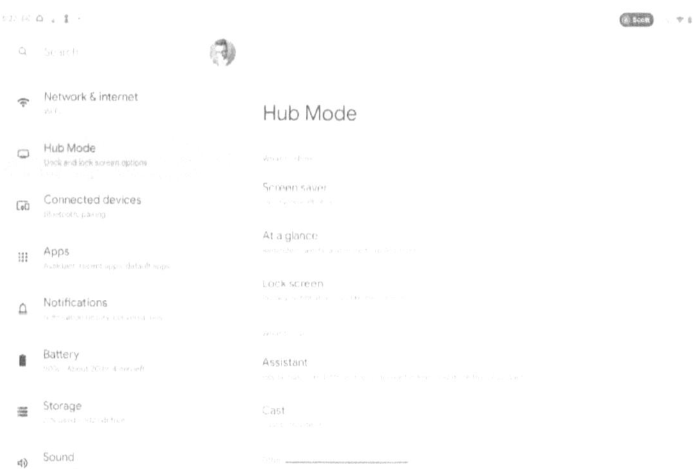

Hub Mode is the mode your tablet is in whenever it is docked to the speaker. It looks like the image below.

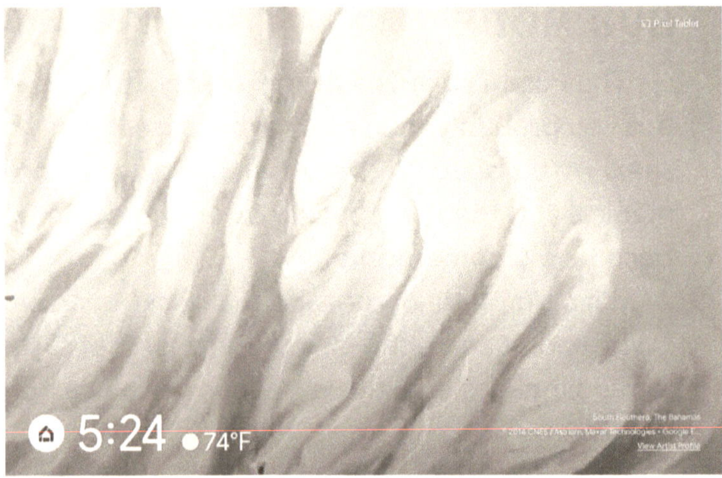

The first thing that you'll probably want to change is the screen saver. Personally, I love the favorite photos one (under Google Photos). I sync my iPhone photos into the Google Photos app; whenever I go into Google Photos and favorite photos (tap the little star on the photo) then it will start rotating into my tablet while it's in Hub Mode.

Not a fan of showing your own photos on the tablet? Then there's plenty of other feature photos and artwork that you can show.

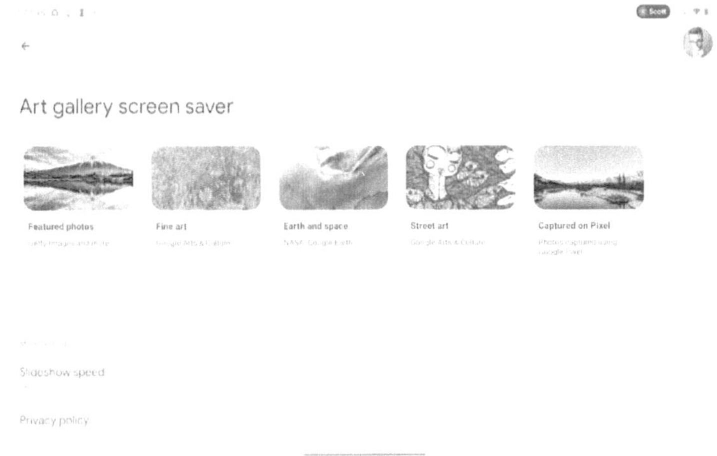

Home settings is where you'll find most of the customizations. If you want to add swipe access to the Google app or add app icons to the home screen, for example, this is where you'll do it.

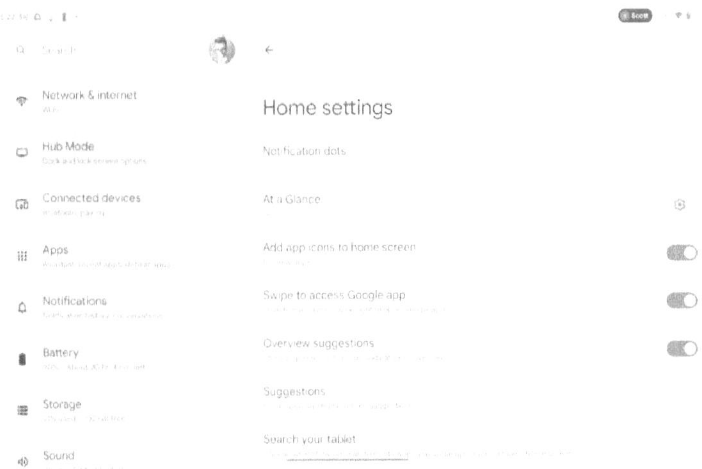

There's also a number of settings in the Lock Settings.

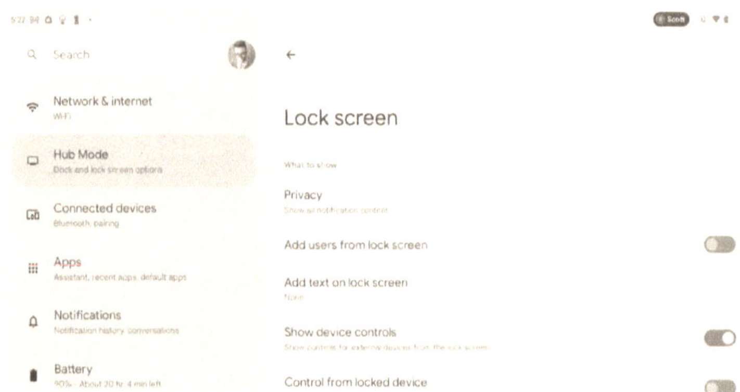

Assistant in Hub Mode isn't too big of a deal if your tablet is in a more private space; but if you keep it out in the open, then there's privacy settings you might want to pay attention to. Who, for example, can ask the Pixel Tablet a question? Only you? Or anyone?

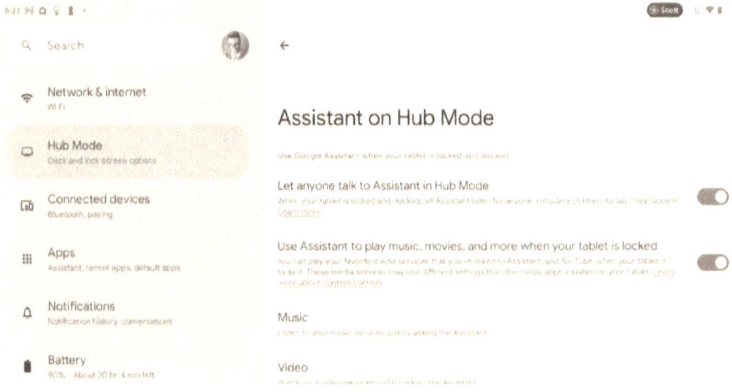

The dock settings has information you might need if you ever need support, but most users will not need to go in here often—if at all.

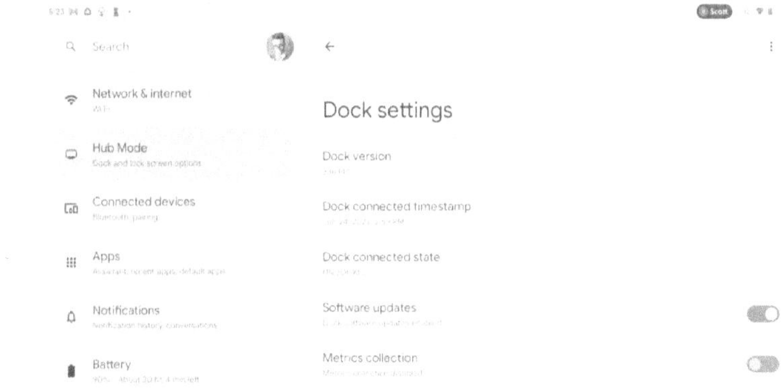

You may have noticed a little home icon on the front of your Pixel Tablet while it's dock. What's that all about?

When you tap it, it will open up your Google Hoe app; this let's you control your house, cameras, and more if you have anything installed. For example, I use cameras and a thermostat; I can see live feeds of the cameras here, as well as adjust my thermostat.

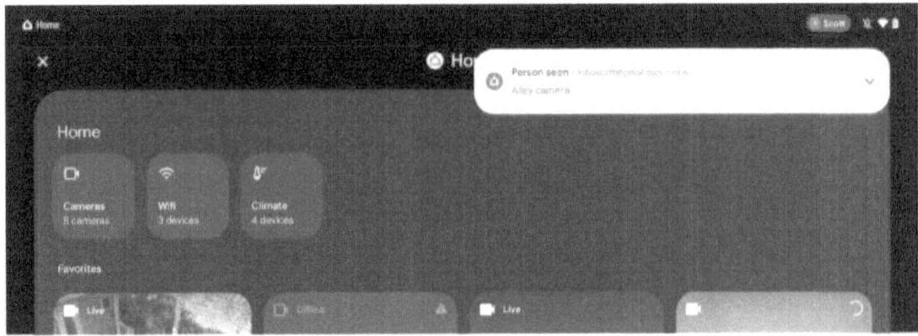

[3]
CUSTOMIZING THE TABLET

MAKING PRETTY SCREENS

If you've used an iPhone or iPad, then you may notice the screen looks a little...bare. There are only a few buttons on it. Maybe you like that. If so, then good for you! Skip ahead. If you want to decorate that screen with shortcuts and widgets, then read on.

ADDING SHORTCUTS

Any app you want on this screen, just find it and then press and hold; when a menu comes up, drag it upward until the screen appears and move it to where you want it to go.

To remove an app from a screen, tap and hold, then tap Remove from the pop-up box.

WIDGETS

Shortcuts are nice, but widgets are better. Widgets are sort of like mini-programs that run on your screen. A common widget people put on their screen is the weather forecast. Throughout the day the widget will update automatically with up-to-date info.

To get started long press on the Canvas area. This brings up a list of options. The one you want is Widgets.

This will show you the most popular widgets, but if you know what you want, then just search for it.

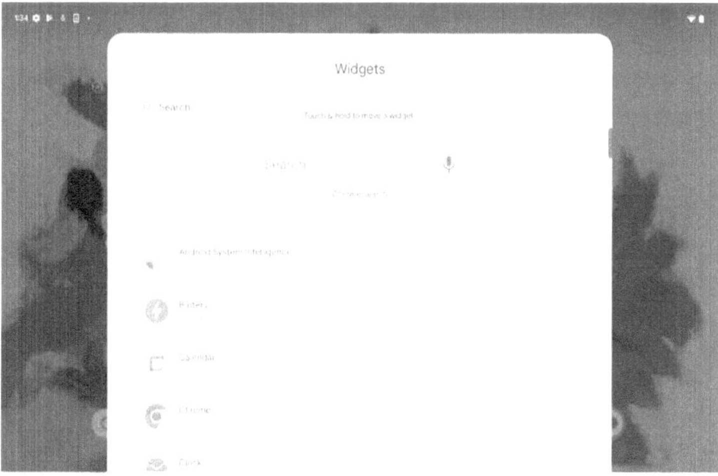

In this example, I'll select the email / Gmail widget, which will let me see email on my canva.

From here, I can drag it where I want it to go and make it bigger or smaller.

To remove a widget just long-press on it until the option menu comes up, and then select remove.

WALLPAPER & STYLES

Adding wallpaper to your screen is done in a similar way. Tap and hold your finger on the Home screen, when the menu comes up, select Wallpaper instead of Widgets.

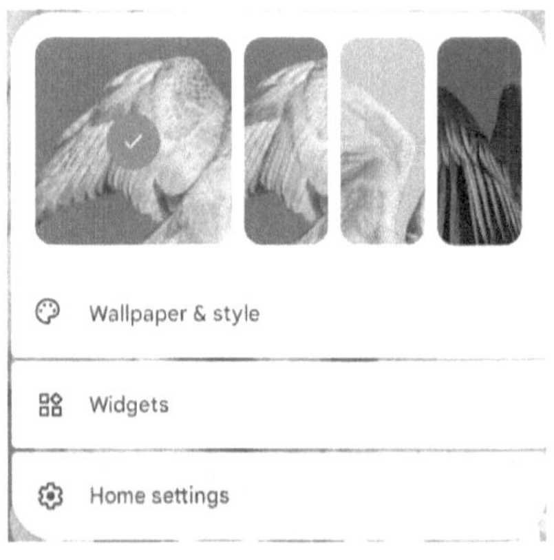

From the Wallpapers menu you have the option to not only change the wallpaper, but also change the style of your tablet—the colors menus and text show on your tablet.

ADDING SCREENS

Adding screens for even more shortcuts and widgets is easy. Tap and hold the Home screen, and swipe to the right.

Next, click the + icon which will add a screen. When you return to your Home screen, you can swipe right and start adding shortcuts and widgets to it.

A WORD, OR TWO, ABOUT MENUS

It's pretty intuitive that if you tap on an icon, it opens the app. What's not so obvious is if you tap and hold there are other options. Every app is different. Usually, they're shortcuts—tapping and holding over the Tablet icon, for example, brings up your favorites; doing the same thing over the camera brings up a selfie mode shortcut. Tap and hold over your favorite apps to see what shortcuts are available.

SPLIT SCREENS

The Google tablet comes in different sizes; a bigger screen obviously gives you a lot more space, which makes split screen apps a pretty handy feature. It works on the smaller Google as well, though it doesn't feel as effective on the smaller screen.

To use this feature, swipe up to bring up multi-tasking; next, tap the icon above the window you want to turn into split screen (note: this feature is not supported on all apps); if split screen is available, you'll see a menu that has an option for split screen.

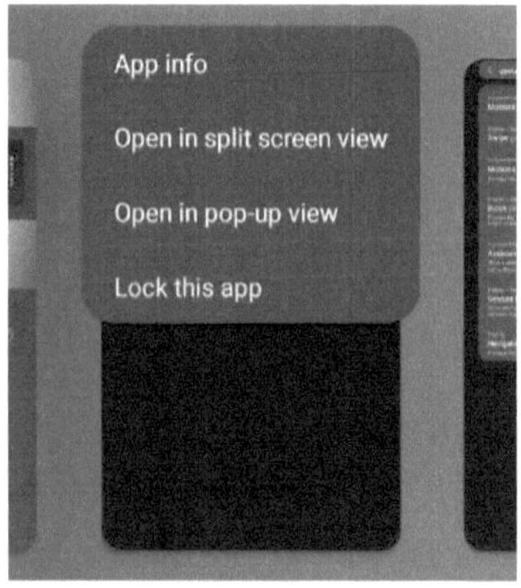

Once you tap split screen, it will let you swipe left and right to find the app you want to split the screen with. Tap the one you want.

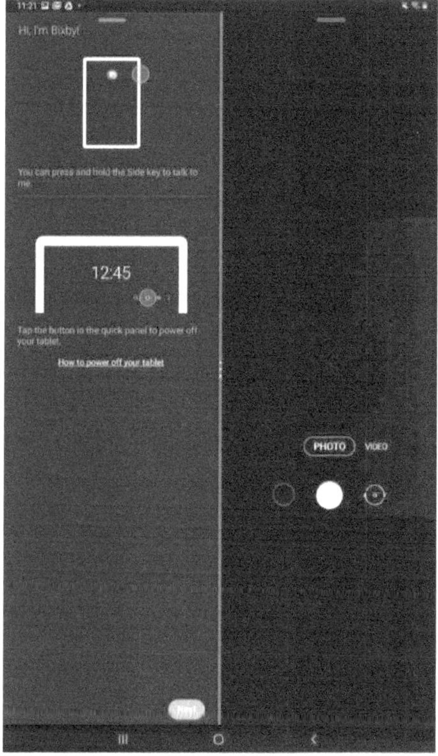

Your screen is now split in two.

That thin blue bar in the middle is adjustable; you can move it up or down so one of the apps has more screen real estate.

To exit this mode, drag the black bar either all the way to the top or all the way to the bottom until one of the apps completely goes away.

[5]

THE BASICS…AND KEEP IT RIDICULOUSLY SIMPLE

Now that you have your tablet set up and know your way around the device at its most basic level, let's go over the apps you'll be using the most.

CONTACTS

Let's open up the Contacts app to get started. See it? It's on your favorites bar, but you can also swipe up to see all your apps and get to it.

It looks like this:

Chances are if you've added your email account, you'll already have a lot of contacts listed. Like hundreds!

You can either search for the contact by clicking the magnifying glass, scroll slowly, or head to the right-hand side of the app and scroll—this lets you quickly scroll by letters. Just slide your finger until you see the letter of the contact you want and then stop.

I'm getting ahead of myself, however! Before you can scroll, it would be nice to know how to add a contact so there are people to scroll to. To add a contact, tap on that plus sign.

Adding a person looks more like applying for a job than adding a contact. There are rows and rows of fields!

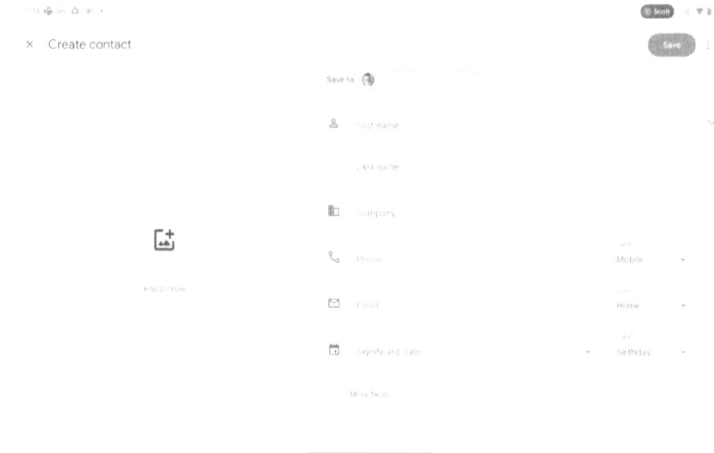

Just in case you weren't overwhelmed by all the fields, you can tap more fields and get even more!

Here's the most important thing you need to know: fields are optional! You can add a name and email and that's it. You don't even have to add their tablet number. If you want to call them, then that would certainly help though.

If you have a hard time remembering who people are, then you can also take a picture or add a picture you already have. Comes in handy if you have eight kids and you can't remember if Joey is the one with blonde hair or red hair. Just tap the camera icon up top, then tap either Gallery (to assign a photo you've already taken) or Camera (to take a picture of them); you can also use one of the avatar type icons Google has.

Once you are done, tap the save button.

EDITING A CONTACT

If you add an email and then later decide you should add a tablet number, or if you want to edit anything else, then just find the name in your contacts and tap it once. This brings up all the info you've already added.

Go to the bottom of the screen and tap on the Edit option button. This makes the contact editable. Go to your desired field and update. When you are finished make sure to tap Save.

SHARING A CONTACT

If you have your tablet long enough, someone will ask you for so-and-so's tablet number. The old-fashioned way was to write it down. But you have a tablet, so you aren't old-fashioned!

The new way to share a number is to find the person in your contacts, tap their name, then tap Share on the bottom left corner of the screen.

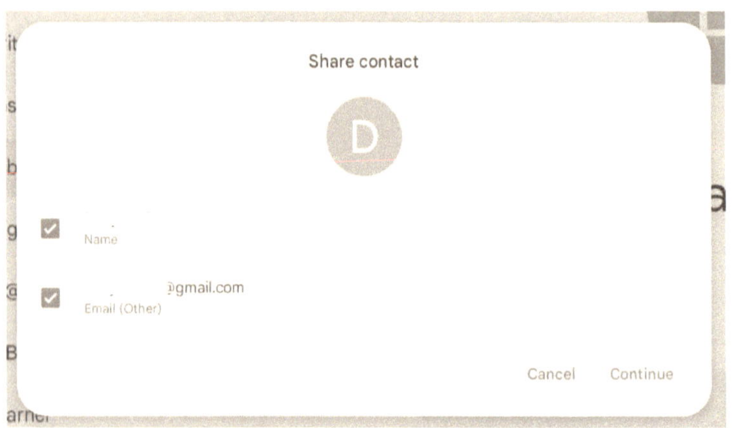

From here you have a few options, but the easiest is to text or email the contact to your friend. This sends them a contact card. So if you have other information with that contact (such as email) then that will be sent over as well.

Delete Contact

Deleting a contact is the same as sharing a contact. The only difference is once you tap their name, you tap the delete icon to the right (not the share to the left). This erases them from your tablet, but not your life.

GET ORGANIZED

Once you start getting lots of contacts, then it's going to make finding someone more time-consuming. Groups helps. You can add a Group for "Family" for instance, and then stick all of your family members there.

When you open your contacts and tap those three lines in the upper left corner, you'll see a menu. This is where you'll see your Groups. So with Groups, you can jump right into that list and find the contact you need.

You can also send the entire group inside the Group an email or text message. So for instance, if your child is turning two and you want to remind everyone in your "Family" contact not to come, then just tap on that Group.

But what if you don't have labels? Or if you want to add people to a label? Easy. Remember that long application you used to add a contact? One of the fields was called "Groups." You have to tap more to see it. It's all the way at the bottom. One of the last fields, in fact.

If you've never added a label or want to add a new one, then just start typing. If you have another one that you'd like to use, then just tap the arrow and select it.

When you are done, don't forget to tap Save.

You can also quickly assign someone to a group by tapping on the contact's name, then selecting Create Group from the upper right.

Once you tap that, you'll get to add a name, assign a ringtone, and assign other members.

DELETE GROUP

If you decide you no longer want to have a label, then just go to the menu I showed you above—side menu, then the three dots. From here, tap the Delete Group.
If there's just one person you want to boot from the label, then tap them and go to the Group and delete it.

MESSAGES

Now that you know how Contacts and the Tablet works, messaging will be like second nature. They share many of the same properties.

Let's open up the Messages app (you have to swipe up and go to all apps). It looks like this:

The first time you open it, you'll have to set it up by scanning the QR code with your phone.

CREATE / SEND A MESSAGE

When you have selected the contact(s) to send a message to, tap Compose. You can also manually type in the number in the text field.

You can add more than one contact—this is known as a group text.

The first time you send a message, it's going to probably look pretty bare like the image below. Assuming you have never sent one, it's going to be blank. Once you start getting messages, you can tap on New category to create labels for them—so all your family messages, for example, will be in one place.

Once you are ready to send your first message, tap the message icon.

The top field is where you put who it's going to (or the group name if it's several people). You can use the + icon to find people in your contacts.

Use the text field to type out your message.

WHERE'S AN APP FOR THAT?

I mentioned earlier that you could play Angry Birds while talking to your angry mom on the tablet. Sound fun? But where is Angry Birds on your tablet? It's not! You have to download it.

Adding and removing apps on the Galaxy is easy. Head to your favorite bar on the bottom of your Home screen and tap the Google Play app.

This launches the Play Store.

From here you can browse the top apps, see editors' picks, look through categories, or, if you have an app in mind, search for it. The Play Store isn't just for apps. You can use the tabs on the top to go to movies, books, and music. Any kind of downloadable content that's offered by Google can be found here.

When you see the app you want, tap on it. You can read through reviews, see screenshots, and install it on your tablet. To install, simply tap the install button—if it's a paid app you'll be prompted to buy it. If there's no price, it's free (or offers in-app payments—which means the app is free, but there are premium features inside it you may have to pay for).

The app is now stored in the app section of your device (remember the section you get to when you swipe up from the bottom to the top?).

Remove App

If you decide you no longer want an app, go to the app in the app menu and tap and hold it. This brings up a box with a few options. The one you want is Uninstall.

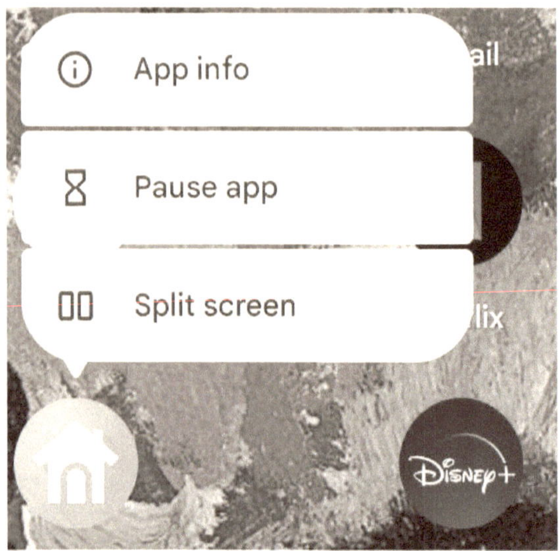

If you downloaded the app from the Play Store, you can always delete it. Some apps that were pre-installed on your tablet cannot be deleted.

You can also go into your settings and delete it. It's in the Apps category.

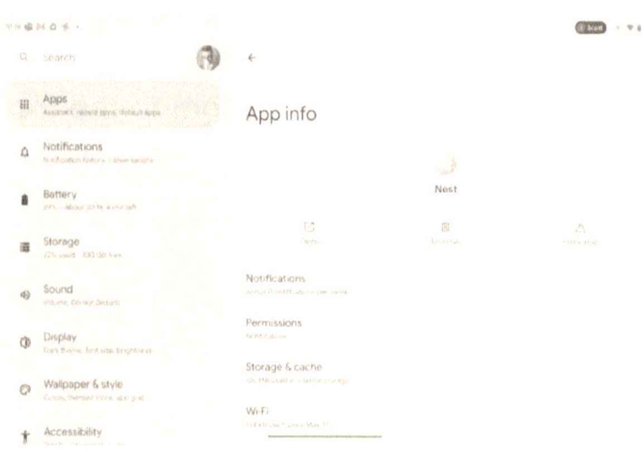

DRIVING DIRECTIONS

Back in the day, you may have had a GPS. It was a fancy plastic device that would give you directions for anywhere in North America. You can throw out that device because your tablet is your new GPS…kind of. Kind of because you need to have some way to get data to your tablet if you don't have wi-fi.

To get directions, swipe up to open up your apps, and go to the Google folder. Tap the Maps app.

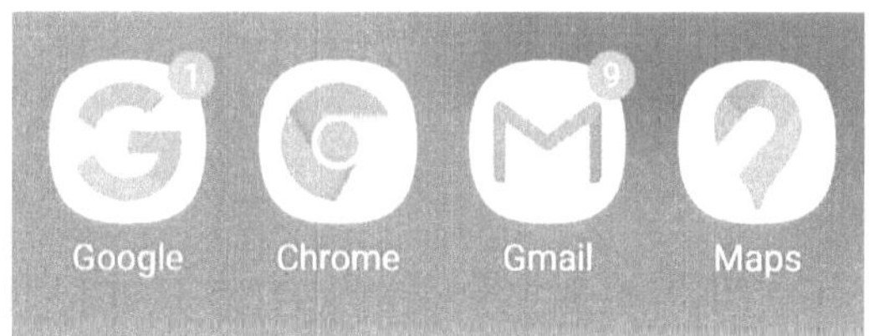

It's automatically going to be set to wherever you are currently at—which is both creepy and useful.

To get started, just type where you want to go. I'm searching for Disneyland, Anaheim.

It automatically starts filling in what it thinks you are going to type and tells you the distance. When you see the one you want, tap it.

It pinpoints the location on the map and also gives you an option to call, share or get directions to the location. If you want to zoom out or in, just use two fingers and pinch in or out on the screen.

It automatically gets directions from where you are. Want it from a different location? Just tap on the "Your location" field and type where you want to go. You can also reverse the directions by tapping on the double arrows. When you are ready to go, tap Start.

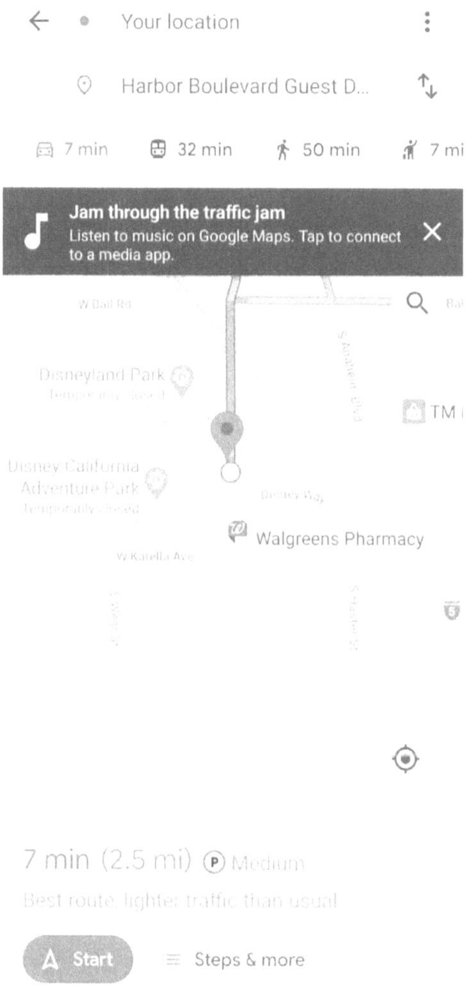

What if you don't want to drive? What if you want to walk? Or bike? Or take a taxi? There are options for all of those and more! Tap the slider under the address bar to whatever you prefer. This updates the directions—when you walk, for example, it will show you one-way streets and also update the time it will take you.

What if you want to drive but are like me: terrified of freeways in California? There's an option to avoid highways. Tap the menu button in the upper right corner of the screen and select Route options (there are actually lots of other things packed in here like adding stops, sharing directions, and sharing your location).

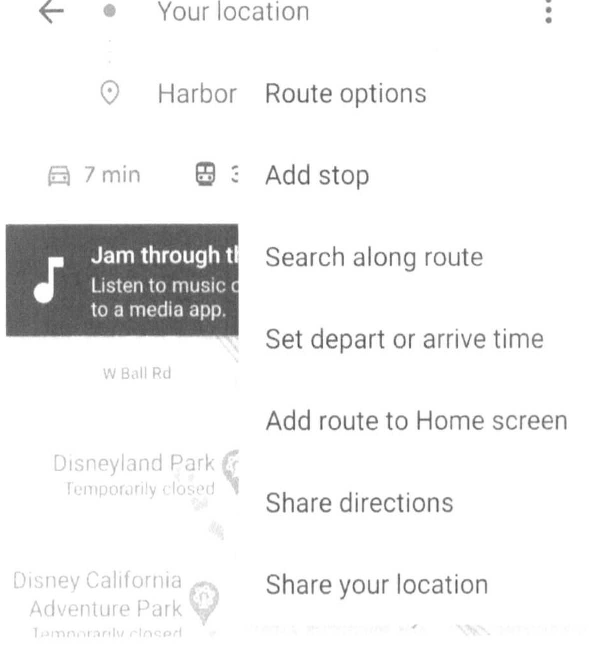

In the Route options, select what you want to avoid, and hit Done. You are now rerouted to a longer route—notice how the times probably changed?

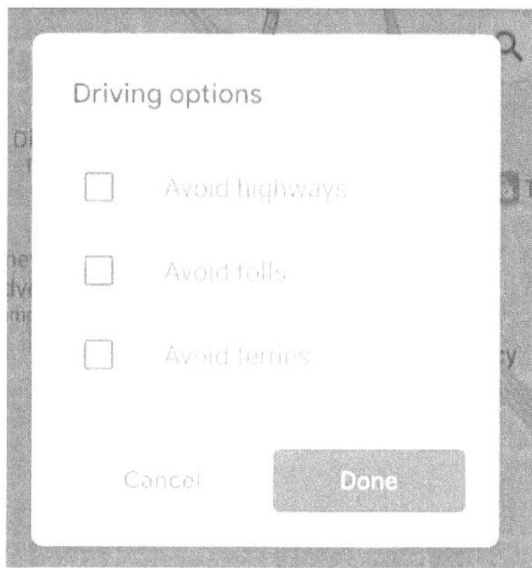

Once you get your directions, you can swipe up to get turn-by-turn directions.

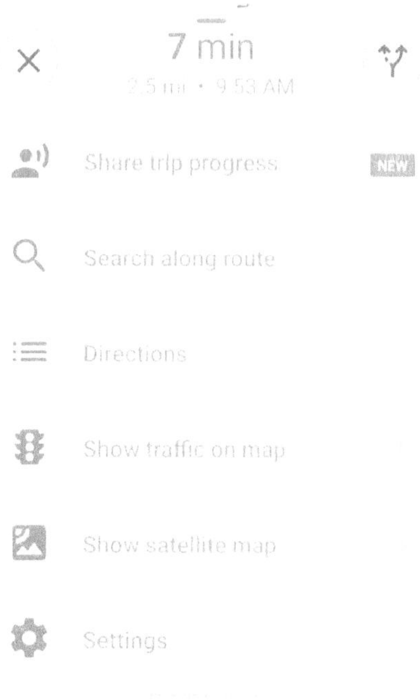

You can even see what it looks like from the street. It's called Street View.

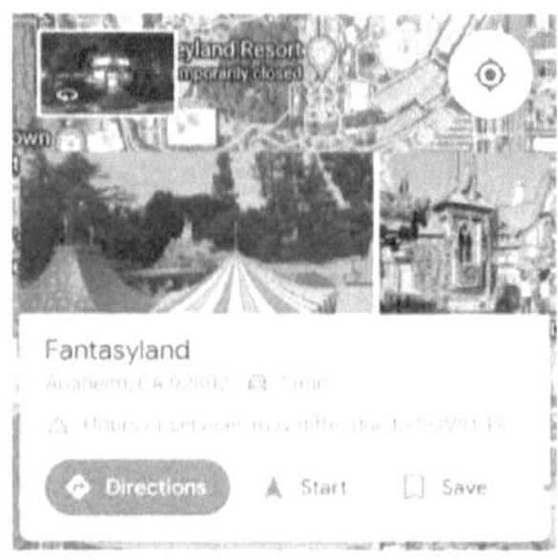

Street View isn't only for streets. Google is expanding the feature everywhere. If you hold your finger over the map, there will be an option to show Street View if it's available. Just tap the thumbnail. Here's a Street View of Disneyland:

You can wander around the entire park! If only you could ride the rides, too! You can get even closer to the action by picking up the Dreamview headset. When you stick your tablet in that, you can turn your head and the view turns with you.

Street View is also available in a lot of malls and other tourist attractions. Point your map to the Smithsonian in Washington, DC and get a pretty cool Street View.

LIVE CAPTIONING

One of the bigger features to Android 10 is live captioning; live captioning can transcribe any video you record and show what's being said. It works surprisingly well and is pretty accurate.

To turn it on, go to Settings > Accessibility > Hearing enhancements > Live caption.

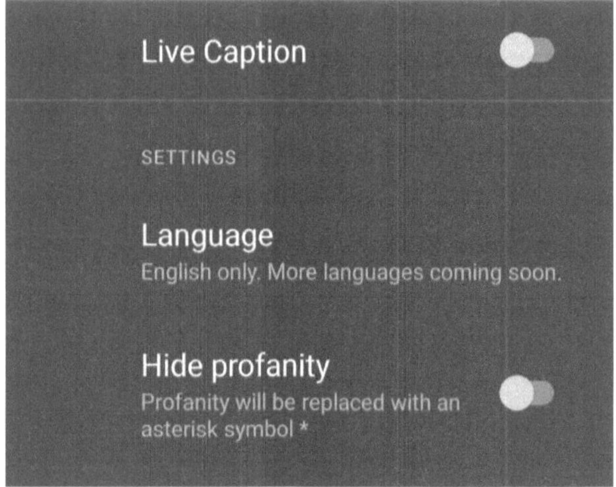

In the settings, you can also toggle off profanity, and, coming soon, select a different language. If it's something you'd only occasionally use, I recommend leaving it toggled off, but having it toggled on under Live Caption in volume control. With that toggled on, all you have to do is press the volume button. Once you do that, you'll see the option to turn it on; it's the bottom option.

Once it's on, you'll start seeing a transcription appear in seconds.

SHARING WI-FI

Anytime you have guests over, you almost always get the question: what's your wi-fi password? If you are like me, then it probably annoys you. Maybe your password is really long, maybe you just don't like giving out your password, or maybe you are just too embarrassed to say that it's "Feet$FetishLover1." Whatever the reason, then you will love sharing your wi-fi with QR codes. Gone are the days of giving this info out. Just give them a code that they scan, and they'll have access without ever knowing what your password is.

To use it, go to your wi-fi settings, then select the Wi-Fi options and Wi-Fi Direct.

Make sure both devices have Wi-Fi on and follow the directions.

[6]
LET'S GO SURFING NOW!

When it comes to the Internet, there are two things you'll want to do:

- Send email
- Browse the Internet

ADD AN EMAIL ACCOUNT

When you set up your tablet, you'll set it up to your Google Account, which is usually your email.

You may, however, want to add another email account—or remove the one you set up.

To add an email, swipe up to bring up your apps, and tap on Settings.

Next, tap on Accounts.

From here, select Add Account; you can also tap on the account that's been set up and tap remove account—but remember you can have more than one account on your tablet.

Once you add your email, you'll be asked what type of email it is. Follow the steps after you select the email type to add in your email, password, and other required fields.

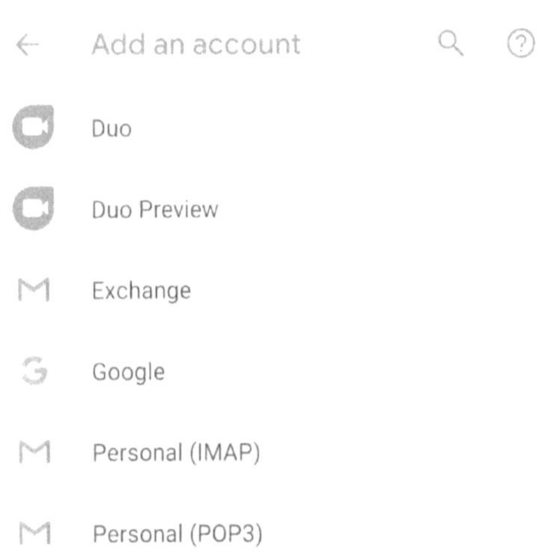

CREATE AND SEND AN EMAIL

To send an email using Gmail (Google's native email app), swipe up to get to your apps, tap Gmail, and tap Compose a New Email (the little round, red pencil in the lower right corner). When you're done, tap the Send button.

You can also use the Google Play Store to find other email apps (such as Outlook).

MANAGE MULTIPLE EMAIL ACCOUNTS

If you have more than one Gmail account, tap the three lines at the upper left of your email screen; this brings out a slider menu. If you tap on the little arrow next to the email address, it drops down and will show other accounts. If none are listed, you can add one.

SURFING THE INTERNET

Google has an Internet browser. It's pretty good. My advice? Use Google Chrome (also on the tablet). The reason is anywhere else you use the Chrome browser (like your desktop or phone) can be sync-d with the tablet.

Get started by tapping on the Chrome browser icon from your favorite bar, or by going into all programs.

If you've used Chrome on a desktop or any other device, then this chapter won't exactly be rocket science—just like the email app, many of the same properties you find on the desktop exist on the mobile version.

When you open it, you'll see it's a pretty basic browser. There are three main things that you'll want to note.

- **Address Bar** - As you would guess, this is where you put the Internet address you want to go to (google.com, for example); what you should understand, however is that this is not just an address bar. This is a search bar. You can use it to search for things just as you would searching for something on Google; when you hit the enter key, it takes you to the Google search results page.

- **Tab Button** (the little plus icon next to each tab)- Because you are limited in space, you don't actually see all your tabs like you would on a normal browser; instead you get a button that tells you how many tabs are open. If you tap it, you can either toggle between the tabs, or swipe over one of the pages to close the tab.

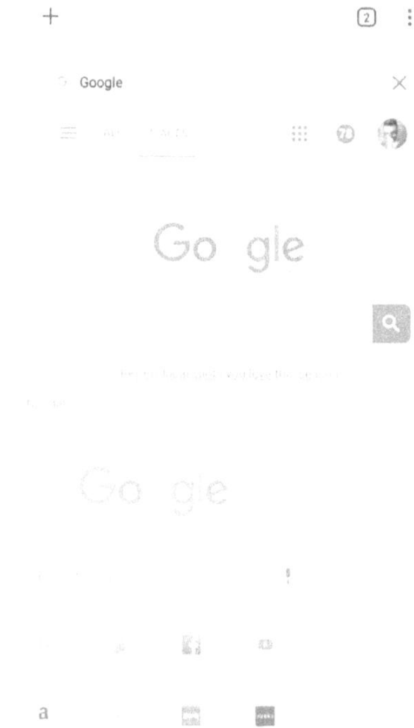

- **Menu Button** - The last button brings up a menu with a series of other options that I'll talk about next.

+ New tab

New Incognito tab

+ New window

History

Downloads

★ Bookmarks

Recent tabs

Share…

Find in page

Add to Home screen

Desktop site

Settings

? Help & feedback

The menu is pretty straightforward, but there are a few things worth noting.

"New incognito tab" opens your tablet into private browsing; that doesn't mean your IP isn't tracked. It means your history isn't record; it also means passwords and cookies aren't stored.

A little bit further down is "History"; if you want your history erased so there's no record on your tablet of where you went, then go here and clear your browsing history.

If you want to erase more than just websites (passwords, for example) then go to Settings at the very bottom of the menu. This opens up more advanced settings.

[7]

SNAP IT!

The camera is the bread and butter of the Google phone. The tablet? Not so much. Yes, it's there; and yes, it's a pretty good camera. But the idea of trying to hold up a large tablet to take a photo is a little cumbersome for most people.

Still, it's nice to occasionally take photos when you are in a bind.

THE BASICS

Are you ready to get your Ansel Adams on? Let's get started by opening the Camera app

When you open the app, it starts in the basic camera mode. The UI can look pretty simple, but don't be fooled. There are a lot of controls.

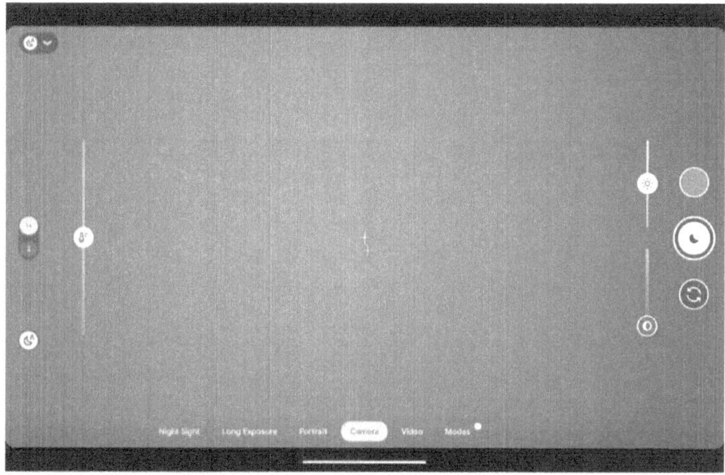

The bottom of the screen has all the commonly used modes: Night Sight (for evening shots), Long Exposure, Portrait (which gives things not in focused a blurred look), Camera, Video, and modes.

Modes has three additional cameras: Panorama, Photo Sphere, and Lens.

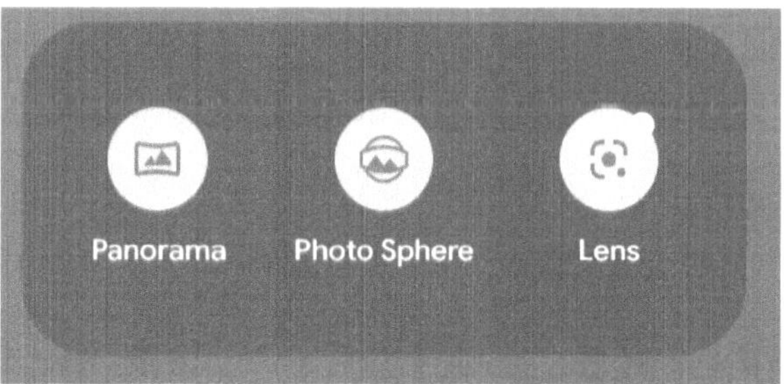

To focus on a subject, just tap it. When you tap on the screen, you'll also see manual controls for brightness, contrast and exposure. If you don't use that, the photo will automatically detect what is best. You can also zoom in by pinching on the screen.

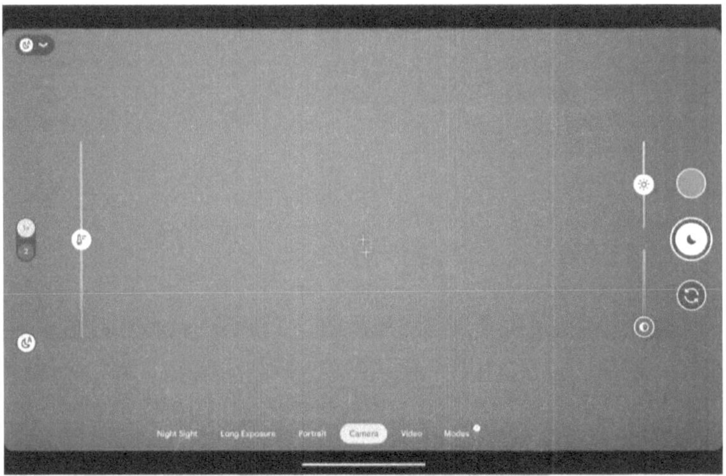

EDITING PHOTOS

Once you take a photo, you can begin fine-tuning it to really make it sparkle. You can access editing by opening the photo you want to make edits to. This is done by either opening it from the camera app by clicking on the photo preview (next to the shutter):

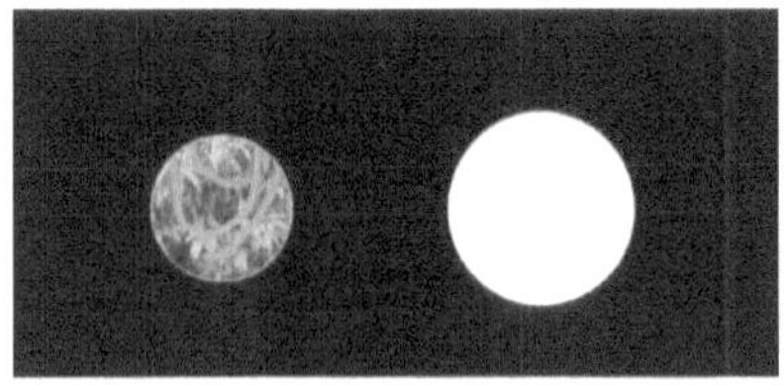

Or by opening the Photo app.

Later in this chapter, I'll write a bit more about how photos are organized, and how you can change things around. For now, we are just talking about editing a photo, so for the purpose of this section, tap on any photo to edit it.

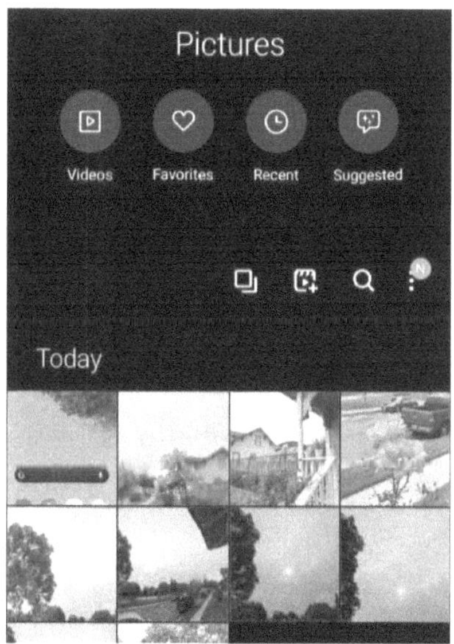

When you open a photo, the options you see will vary depending on what kind of photo you open.

The below example is a Live Focus photo.

As the name suggests, the background is blurred. There's also an option here: Change background effect. This technically isn't editing a photo—when you edit a photo, you go into a different app.

When you tap change the background, you'll have four options. With each option, you can change the intensity of the blur with the slider.

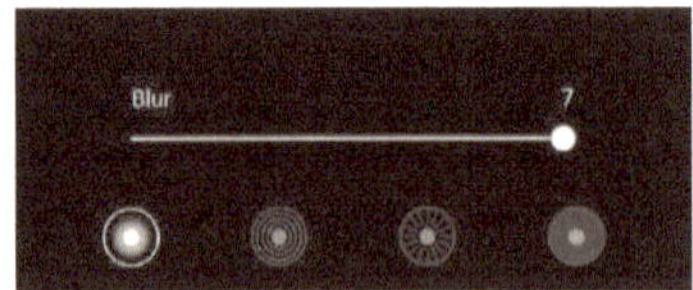

The main blur is simply called "blur"; the next is a spin blur.

The third is a zoom blur.

The last type of blur is color point, which makes the object color and the background black and white.

If you make any changes here, always make sure and tap Apply to save it.

Regardless of the type of photo, there are going to be several options that are the same. Starting on the top, that little play icon will wirelessly show your photo on another device (like a compatible TV).

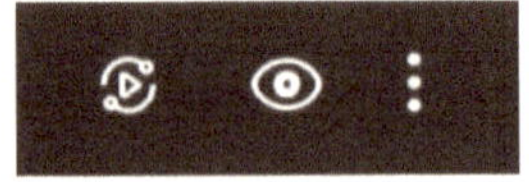

Next to the play icon is an icon that looks kind of like an eye. That will digitally scan your photo and try and identify what the photo is. In the below example, it finds a flower and gives a link to see more. This feature works pretty well, but isn't always perfect.

Next to the eye icon is an option icon. This will let you set a photo as wallpaper, print it, etc. If you tap Details, it will also let you see when the photo was taken, its resolution, and any tags that have been assigned to it.

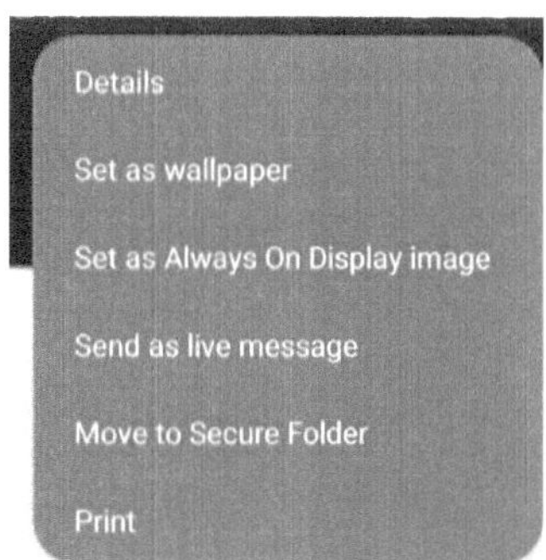

On the bottom of any photo are four additional options. The heart icon favorites the photo, the pencil lets you edit it (more on that in a second), the three dots lets you share it, and the trash lets you delete it.

Tap the pencil icon and let's see how to edit a photo next. Regardless of the photo, you'll see the same options on the bottom.

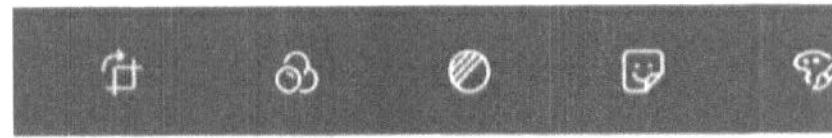

The first option is to crop the photo. To crop, drag the little white corners.

Next is the filter option. The slider lets you select the type of filter, and below that is a slider to adjust the intensity of the filter.

Brightness is the next icon. Each icon here adjusts a different setting (such as the contrast of the photo).

The sticker icon will launch Bitmoji (I'll discuss this later in the chapter), but what this does is let you put stickers on top of your photo.

The paintbrush icon lets you draw on top of your photo.

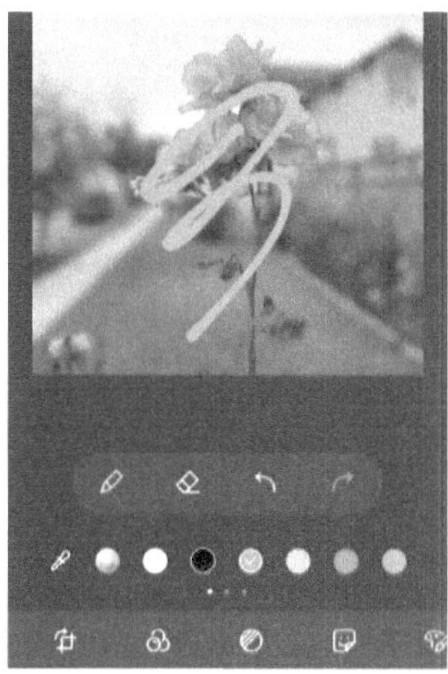

And the text icon lets you write on top of your photo.

If you don't want to spend time editing your photo—you just want it to magically look better with no effort, there's an option up in the upper left corner that will do that for you—it crops, rotates, and adds a filter to it. Depending on how well you took the shot, you may not see much difference.

In the upper right corner is an options menu with even more choices for editing your picture.

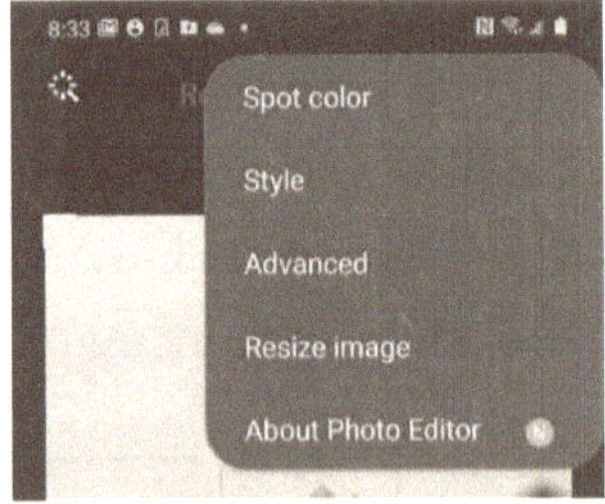

The first is Spot color. Using the little pickers, you can remove a color from the photo to make the subject stand out. To save any changes here, make sure and tap the checkmark; to cancel changes, tap the X.

Style applies filters that give the photo more of an artistic pop—if you want your photo to look like a painting, for example. The slider below it will adjust the intensity.

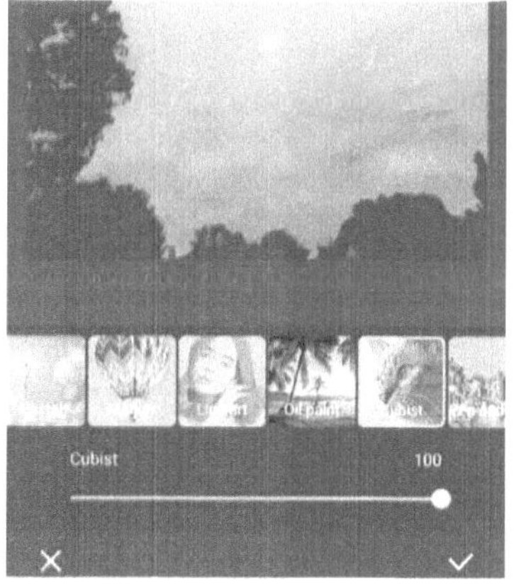

The advanced option will let you do color corrections.

If you took a photo at the highest resolution and are having difficulty sharing it, you can use the Resize image option to make it smaller.

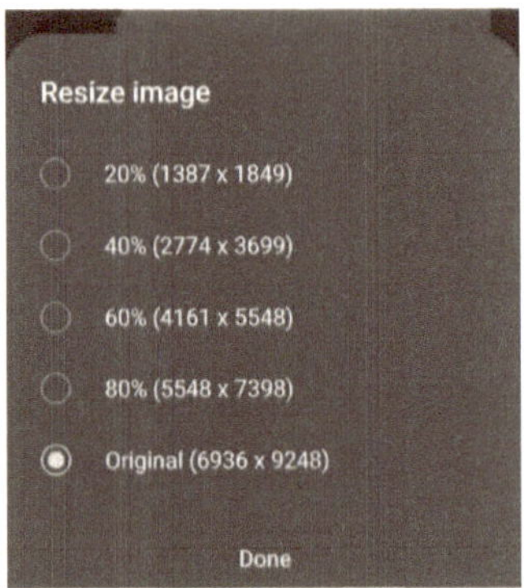

Once you are finished doing edits, make sure and tap Save.

EDITING VIDEOS

Editing a video shares a lot of common features to photos, so make sure and read that section first, as I will not repeat features already referenced above.

To get started open the video that you want to edit, then tap to play it. In the play window, there are going to be a couple of things you should note.

You'll notice the video has the same options at the bottom of it (assuming you haven't played it). To edit it, just tap on that pencil.

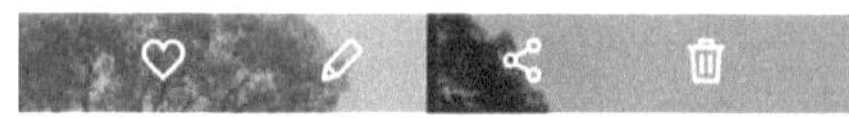

The first option you'll see is to crop the video. To crop just drag in or out the white bars before and after the video clip.

Next is the color filter, which works almost identically to the photo filter.

The text icon comes after this and lets you write on top of the photo.

The emoji sticker insert is after this.

And the paintbrush is second to last.

The last icon is for adding sound. You can add music or anything else you want. You can also use the slider under Video sound to make the videos original sound softer (or nonexistent)—so, for example, you could remove all sound from a family dinner, and replace it with music.

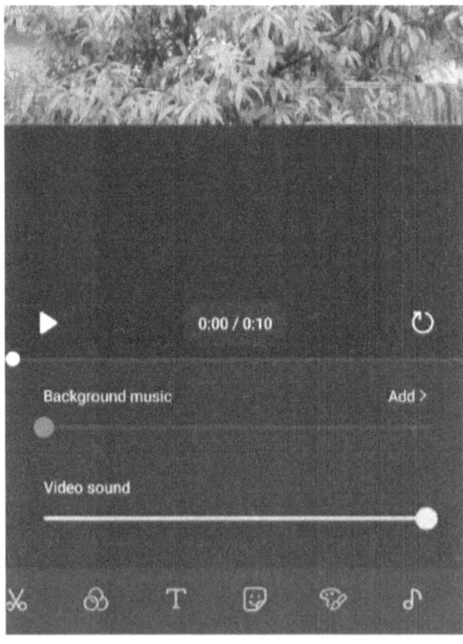

Up on top, there's one option: resolution. If you've recorded in a large format and it's too large, you can use this option to make it smaller.

ORGANIZING YOUR PHOTOS AND VIDEOS

The great thing about mobile photos is you always have a camera ready to capture memorable events; the bad thing about mobile photos is you always have a camera ready to capture events, and you'll find you have hundreds and hundreds of photos very quickly.

Fortunately, Google makes it very simple to organize your photos so you can find what you are looking for.

Let's open up the Photo app and see how to get things organized.

Google keeps things pretty simple by having only four options on the bottom of your screen.

[8]

GOING BEYOND

This chapter will cover:
- System settings

If you want to take total control of your Google, then you need to know where the system settings are and what can and can't be changed there.

First, the easy part: the system settings are located with the rest of your apps. Swipe up and scroll down to "Settings."

This opens all the settings available:
- Network & Internet

- Hub Mode
- Connected Devices
- Apps
- Notifications
- Battery
- Storage
- Sound
- Display
- Wallpaper & Style
- Accessibility
- Security & Privacy
- Location
- Passwords and accounts
- Digital Wellbeing & Parental Controls
- Google
- System
- About Tablet
- Tips and Support

I'll cover what each setting does in this chapter. There's a lot of settings! Need to find something quickly? Use the magnifying glass up top. Before looking at the settings, however, tap the avatar of the person in the upper right corner. That's going to let you add in personal information.

NETWORK & INTERNET

This setting, like most settings, does exactly what it sounds like: it manages how things connect to the Internet, Bluetooth, and data usage.

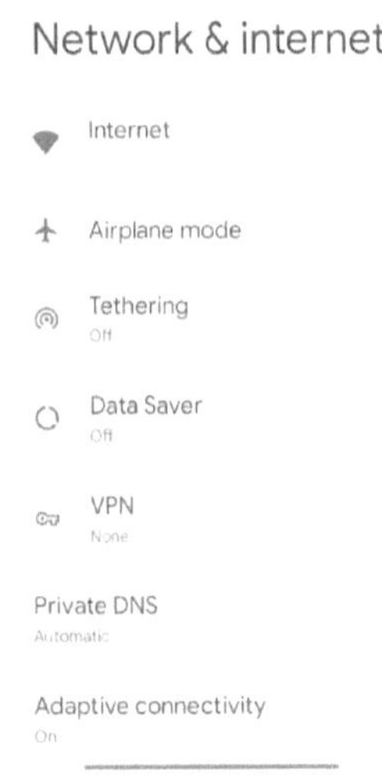

Data usage tells you how much data you've used; tapping on it gives you a deeper overview, so you can see exactly which apps used the data. Why is this important? For most, it probably won't be. I'll give an example of when it helped me: I work on the go a lot; I use the wireless on my tablet to connect my laptop (which is called tethering); my MacBook was set to back up to the cloud, and little did I know it was doing this while connecting to my tablet...20GB later, I was able to pinpoint what happened by looking at the data.

Airplane mode is next. This setting turns off all wireless activity with a switch. So if you're flying and they tell you to turn everything wireless off, you can do it with a switch.

Finally, More connection settings is for doing some wireless connecting on a private network. This is not something a beginning user would need to do, and I'm not going to cover it, as the point of this book is to keep it ridiculously simple. You can also set up wireless printing and wireless emergency alerts here.

CONNECTED DEVICES

Connected devices is where any Bluetooth device will go up; from here you can review, manage, and deleted anything connected to your tablet.

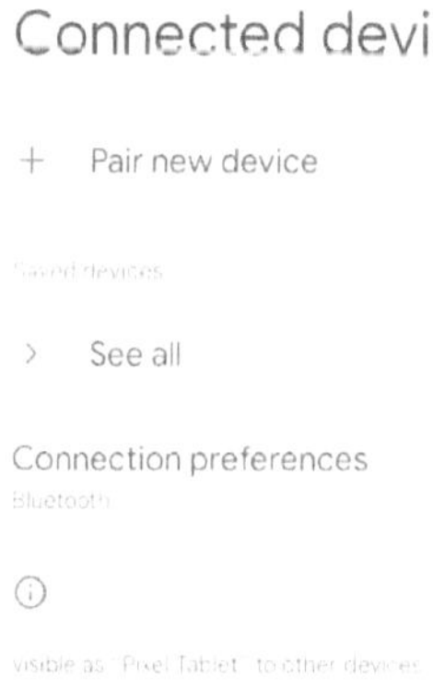

APPS

Every app you download has different settings and permissions. A map app, for example, needs your permission to know your location. You can turn these permissions on and off here. Does it really matter? App makers can't abuse it, right? Sort of. Here's an example: a few months ago, a popular ride-sharing app made headlines because it wanted to know where passengers were after they left the ride, so they could promote different restaurants and stores and make even more money. Many felt this was both greedy and an invasion of privacy; if you are of the latter stance, then you could go in here and stop sharing your location.

How? Just tap Advanced then look at all the permissions you are giving away. Go to the permission you are concerned with and toggle the app from on to off.

Apps

Recently opened apps

Camera
1 min. ago

Google
1 min. ago

Kids Space
3 min. ago

Messages
5 min. ago

> See all 71 apps

NOTIFICATIONS

Notifications are those pop-ups that give you alerts—like new text messages or emails. In the notification setting you can turn them off for some apps while leaving them on for others. You can also enable Do not disturb mode, which will silence all notifications.

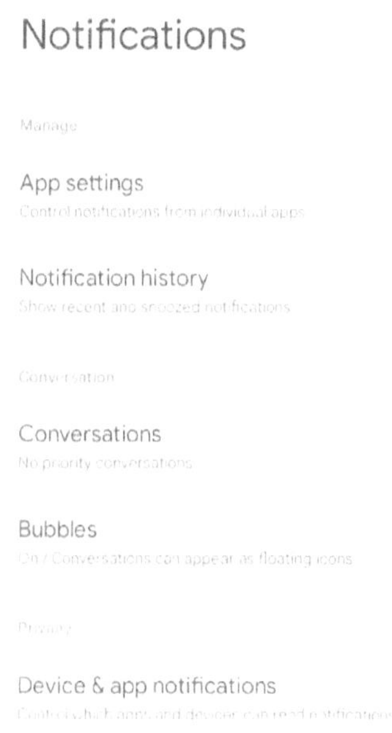

BATTERY

Battery gives you information about your battery health (such as how much of a charge it can hold and how much life it has in hours until it's drained). You can also manage battery saving tactics, such as battery saver.

Battery

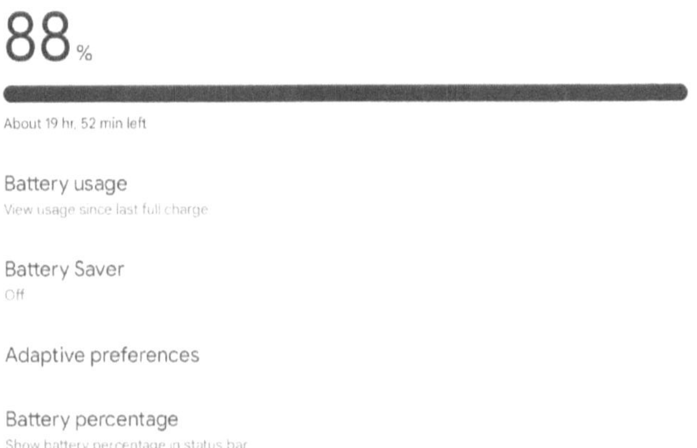

88 %

About 19 hr, 52 min left

Battery usage
View usage since last full charge

Battery Saver
Off

Adaptive preferences

Battery percentage
Show battery percentage in status bar

STORAGE

Storage lets you see how much space you have used and also gives you the ability to free up space if you are running low.

Storage

28 GB used   128 GB total

Free up space
Go to Files app to manage and free up space

System   14 GB

Apps   11 GB

Images   85 MB

Trash   0 B

SOUNDS AND VIBRATIONS

There's a volume button on the side of your tablet, so why would you need to open up a setting for it?! This setting lets you get more specific about your volume.

Sound

Media volume

Call volume

Ring & notification volume

Alarm volume

Do Not Disturb
Off

For example, you may want your alarm to ring super loud in the morning, but you want your music to play very low.

You can also use these settings to adjust the intensity of vibrations.

DISPLAY

As with many of the settings, almost all the main features of the Display setting can be changed outside of the app (in the notifications drop-down, for example).

This is where you'll be able to toggle on dark mode, adjust the brightness, turn on adaptive brightness, and toggle blue light on and off.

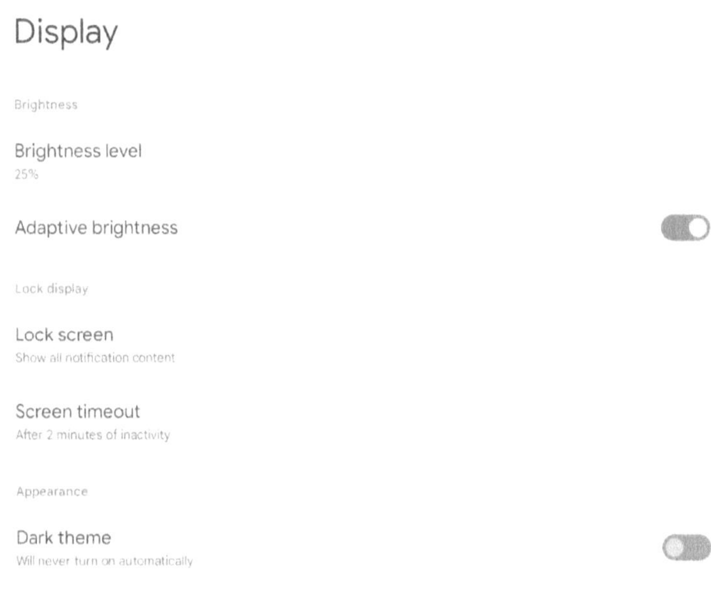

ACCESSIBILITY

Do you hate tablets because the text is too small, the colors are all wrong, you can't hear anything? Or something else? That's where accessibility can help. This is where you make changes to the device to make it easier on your eyes or ears.

Accessibility lets you change things like color and motion on your tablet; it's great if you need things bigger, want things read back to you, and more.

Accessibility

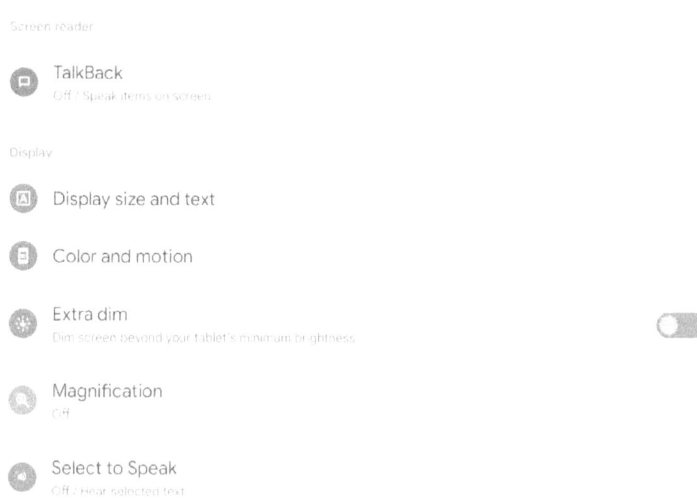

SECURITY AND PRIVACY

If you want to add a fingerprint or an additional person to Face ID, you can do so in this menu. You can also update your own—if you didn't do it with glasses, for example, then go here to redo it.

Like Location Control (covered below), Privacy settings got a big upgrade in Android 10. It's so big, it now fills an entire section in the settings.

The biggest upgrade is the ability to customize what apps see what; it's no longer all or nothing. You can refine exactly how much or how little each app can see.

Tap on Permissions as one example of what you can control.

Security & privacy

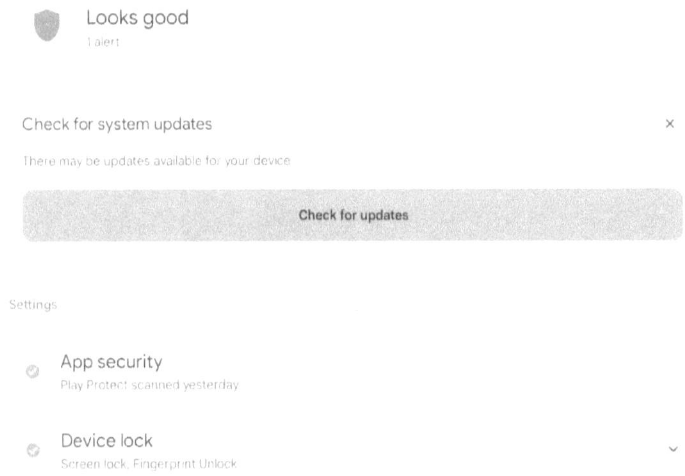

LOCATION

In the past, Location Control was an all or nothing feature—you'd decide if an app could see you all the time or none of the time. That's nice for privacy, but not nice for when you actually need someone to know your location—like when you are getting picked up by a ride app like Lyft. The new Android OS adds a new option for while you are using the app. So, for example, a ride app can only see your location while you are using the app; once the ride is over, they can no longer see what you are doing.

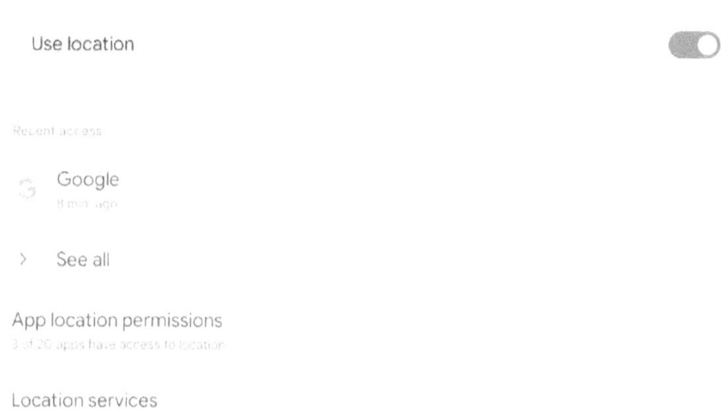

Location

Use location

Recent access

Google
8 min. ago

> See all

App location permissions
3 of 20 apps have access to location

Location services

PASSWORD AND ACCOUNTS

If you have more than one Google account, you can tap on this to add it. If you want to remove your current account, tap on it and tap Remove—remember, however, you can have more than one account. Don't remove it just so you can add another.

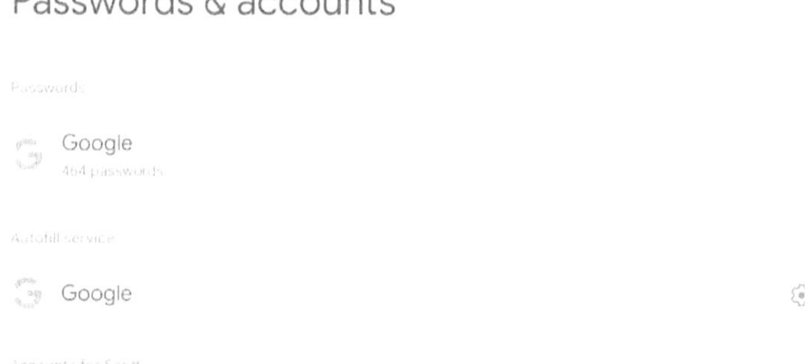

Passwords & accounts

Passwords

Google
464 passwords

Autofill service

Google

Accounts for Scott

You can also use this area to manage all the passwords you have saved on apps.

GOOGLE

Google is where you will go to manage any Google device connected with your tablet. If you are using a Google watch, for example, or a Chromecast.

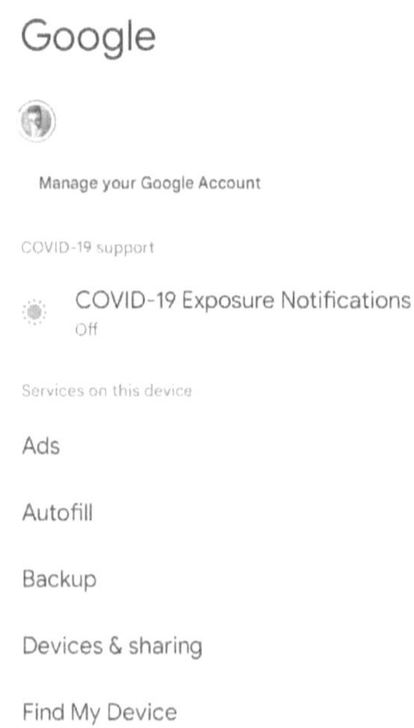

DIGITAL WELLBEING AND PARENTAL CONTROLS

Digital Wellbeing is my least favorite feature on the Google tablet; now when my wife says, "You spend too much time on your tablet"—she can actually prove it! The purpose of the setting is to help you manage your time more. It lets you know you're spending 12 hours a day updating your social media with memes of cats, and "hopefully" make you feel like perhaps you shouldn't do that.

Digital Wellbeing & parental controls

If you have kids using your tablet, this is where you can also set up parental controls.

GENERAL MANAGEMENT

System is where you go to change the language and date / time; the most important thing here, however, is Reset. This is where you can do a complete factory reset of your tablet.

If there's an update available, you would also see it here.

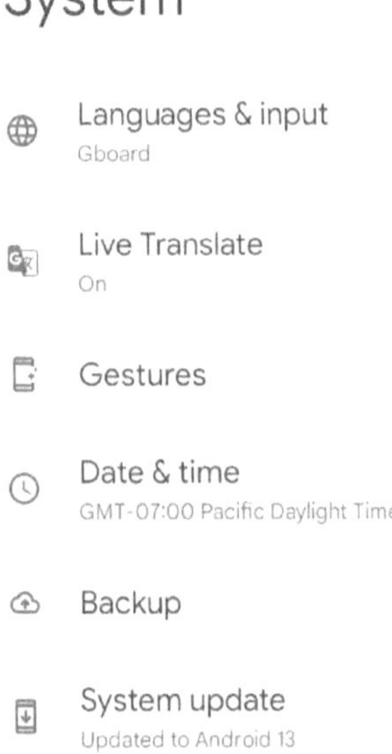

TIPS & SUPPORT

This isn't really a setting. It's just tips and support. You can also talk with support here.

ABOUT TABLET

This is where you will find general information about your tablet. It's more of an FYI, but there are a few settings here that you can change.

INDEX

ABOUT THE AUTHOR

Scott La Counte is a librarian and writer. His first book, *Quiet, Please: Dispatches from a Public Librarian* (Da Capo 2008) was the editor's choice for the Chicago Tribune and a Discovery title for the Los Angeles Times; in 2011, he published the YA book The N00b Warriors, which became a #1 Amazon bestseller; his most recent book is *#OrganicJesus: Finding Your Way to an Unprocessed, GMO-Free Christianity* (Kregel 2016).

He has written dozens of best-selling how-to guides on tech products.

You can connect with him at ScottDouglas.org.

www.ingramcontent.com/pod-product-compliance
Lightning Source LLC
Chambersburg PA
CBHW051221160726
47994CB00002B/700